# A Concise Guide to Community Planning

Gerald A. Porterfield

Kenneth B. Hall, Jr.

McGraw-Hill, Inc.

New York   San Francisco   Washington, D.C.   Auckland   Bogotá
Caracas   Lisbon   London   Madrid   Mexico City   Milan
Montreal   New Delhi   San Juan   Singapore
Sydney   Tokyo   Toronto

**Library of Congress Cataloging-in-Publication Data**

Porterfield, Gerald A.
    A concise guide to community planning / Gerald A. Porterfield,
Kenneth B. Hall, Jr.
        p.    cm.
    Includes bibliographical references and index.
    ISBN 0-07-025591-1 (acid-free paper)
    1. City planning—United States.    2. Regional planning—United
States. 3. Community development—United States    I. Hall, Kenneth
B.    II. Title.
HT167.P67    1994
307.1'216'0973—dc20                                                94-13942
                                                                              CIP

        4 5 6 7 8 9 0    DOH/DOH    9 0 9


ISBN 0-07-025591-1


*The sponsoring editor for this book was Joel Stein, the editing supervisor was
Jane Palmieri, and the production supervisor was Pamela Pelton. It was set in
Times Roman by McGraw-Hill's Professional Book Group composition unit.*

*Printed and bound by R. R. Donnelley & Sons Company.*


This book is printed on acid-free paper.

*To our wives, without whom nothing would be possible.*

# Contents

# Preface

## Setting the Stage

Community planning will be one of the most important urban design issues in the 1990s because it affects every element of our society. In post-World War II America it became possible for many to realize the dream of owning a home in the suburbs. Land was plentiful and ecological issues were as yet unrecognized.

During the 1950s, the movement of the population away from concentrated urban centers to the countryside led to the evolution of the suburban residential neighborhood, and ultimately to strip commercial development. The demand for lower density and privacy resulted in the consumption of large tracts of land at the expense of the environment and the social structure of the community at large. Unfocused planning and laissez-faire attitudes between burgeoning municipalities and land developers resulted in the chaotic situation we now refer to as *sprawl*. The proliferation of the automobile compounded this situation by increasing the distances that could be easily traversed as our society pursued the basic requirements of daily life: employment, food, shelter, and recreation.

The baby boomers born in this era were responsible for the increase in social consciousness of the 1960s and 1970s. This same group has matured and, as today's consumers, are demanding a higher standard of design for the communities in which they live. It is not enough to own one's own home; the community in which it is located must have a unique character and a sense of place, and it must be environmentally responsible. The urban sprawl, which resulted from unchecked and undirected development in recent decades, is giving way to development that is both economically feasible and marketable. The challenge of the 1990s and beyond is to accommodate the kind of growth that instills a sense of community identity through effective design solutions that deal with the conundrum of continuing urban development.

This process is complicated by environmental issues, which continue to gain momentum in public awareness, not only in this country but the world over. The debate over global warming, ozone depletion, and water and air quality, as well as our own national considerations regarding wetlands, habitat preservation, old-growth forest protection, and metropolitan growth controls are promising to be formidable challenges to designers and planners well into the next millennium. Stewardship of the earth's resources is no longer a lofty ideal to work toward; it is a mandate that must influence our decision-making process.

Garden cities, new towns, and planned unit developments each were espoused in their time as exemplary patterns for new growth and development. Indeed, each contributed partial solutions to the problems inherently associated with growth, but they also contributed to the problem. Requiring large tracts of land to accommodate a variety of housing types and commercial activities, usually they were situated on the periphery of urbanized areas. In addition, the majority of these types of developments provided at best only minimal opportunities for employment. Long commutes required residents to endure increased traffic congestion and the abandonment of the residential area during the working hours, relegating such areas to bedroom community status. In effect, they were sprawl.

Currently, the newly rediscovered concept embodied in neotraditionalist villages serves as a field experiment for the serious student of community design. This concept attempts to reduce the need for the automobile by centralizing life's necessities within walking distance of housing, thereby appealing to the nostalgia for past decades. The reduced scale of the towns, reminiscent of the late nineteenth and early twentieth centuries, addresses the newly kindled desire to escape the gridlock of crowded highways and return to a simpler lifestyle. It seeks to provide the consumer with an alternative to typical suburbia by increasing opportunities for interaction among neighbors that embody the concept of community.

However, new philosophies must not overlook the mandate to provide an efficient and sensitive framework for growth for our existing towns and cities. Urban planners and public officials must redefine growth parameters, in not only the evolving urban centers of the future but the metropolitan centers of today. The continuing struggle between pro-growth and no-growth advocates underlines this need. Sense of place, the heart and soul of community character and identity, can be achieved only through deliberate action in the planning process. True communities do not just occur; they are shaped.

A cooperative effort between the public and private sectors is necessary if we are to ensure the success of our planning process. Community design is not the domain of a single professional group. It is the responsibility of all professions that participate in the process. Landscape architects, architects, engineers, municipal planners, elected officials, and land developers all bear responsibility. Because of the increased awareness of environmental issues and the negative economic ramifications of uncontrolled growth, the myopia of professional rivalry and political expediency have no place in this process if we are to effect lasting changes in our towns and cities.

The tools for this task are already in place in the form of an existing system of site plan, subdivision, and zoning regulations. However, this system's flaw is that it offers guidelines for solutions that are only minimally acceptable, rather than requiring the very best. Indeed, these regulations, in conjunction with the explosion of national commercial chain stores, has in essence created *franchised* cities and towns across America. The essential character of many communities has been lost, making it almost impossible to distinguish one region of the country from another. If we take positive steps now to establish a framework, we can achieve the changes that are necessary to bring about a stronger sense of community and develop a broader vision than that attained in parcel-by-parcel growth. By definition, growth in and of itself is good, as it usually signifies economic vitality and financial health. Where effective master plans for growth are implemented, balanced economic expansion is more apt to be realized, assuring a larger tax base from which the community as a whole benefits. Where no vision for growth exists, sprawl results.

We must be proactive in effecting change, rather than merely reactive to these issues as they emerge. The diversity of housing options, shopping and employment opportunities, recreation and open space, as well as our varied forms of transportation are the building blocks of our communities. In themselves they do not solely embody the image of the community, but in combination they can reflect either balanced, sensitive forethought or an undefined, built environment with missed opportunities. It is to this task that we as community planners must attend if growth is to be responsible.

*Gerald A. Porterfield*
*Kenneth B. Hall, Jr.*

# Acknowledgments

We wish to acknowledge the publishers and authors of the following publications for their kind permission to use their work as resources for this book.

1. *Garden Cities of Tomorrow* (1973), by Ebenezar Howard, published by the M.I.T. Press, Cambridge, Mass.

2. *Merriam-Webster's Collegiate Dictionary,* Tenth Edition (1993), by Merriam-Webster Inc., Springfield, Mass., publisher of Merriam-Webster dictionaries.

3. *City Lights, An Introduction to Urban Studies* (1981), by E. Barbara Phillips and Richard T. LeGates, published by Oxford University Press, New York.

4. *A History of Landscape Architecture: The Relationship of People to the Environment* (1973), by George B. Tobey, originally published by the American Elsevier Publishing Company, Inc., and now distributed by Books on Demand, a division of University Microfilms International, Ann Arbor, Mich.

5. *The Image of the City* (1960), by Kevin Lynch, published by The M.I.T. Press, Cambridge, Mass.

6. *The Social Life of Small Urban Spaces* (1980), by William H. Whyte, originally published by The Conservation Foundation and now distributed by Books on Demand, a division of University Microfilms International, Ann Arbor, Mich.

7. *The Life and Death of Great American Cities* (1961), by Jane Jacobs, published by Random House, Inc., New York.

8. *Site Planning,* Second Edition (1962), by Kevin Lynch published by The M.I.T. Press, Cambridge, Mass.

9. *A Visual Approach to Park Design* (1981), by Albert Rutledge, published by Garland Publishing Inc., New York.

# Introduction

Community planners come from many professions and bring many years of training and experience to their task. Each profession approaches the challenges of growth from a unique perspective. Community planning has never been identified as the sole domain of any one profession, as many significant contributions from each have been recognized. While there are examples of cooperation among the contributing professions, there are probably an equal number of instances of an unwillingness to compromise because of professional rivalry. Good community planning can be accomplished only through teamwork; and teamwork can be achieved only through an understanding of the importance of the role of each member and a common respect for the part that each can play in the process.

It is the goal of this book to provide designers and planners with an easy-to-comprehend handbook that can be used daily for an overview of land development issues and practical alternative design strategies. The information included in each chapter provides a resource for realistic approaches to community planning that will take the user step-by-step through the design process. This is not intended to be the last word on the subject, but should be used as a technical supplement to the many reference works already in publication. The theory, practical applications, and examples provide a format that can be used by anyone involved in community planning, whether by the seasoned professional as a compendium or by the beginner as a tool for understanding the profession. Although planning policy varies throughout the country, this book will attempt to provide a framework for cooperation among the professions by providing some practical design solutions to common problems faced by all.

We as authors assume that the reader currently is a participant in the community planning process, or is preparing to enter one of the professions associated with it. Whether one is a landscape architect, land planner, engineer, architect, municipal planner, elected official, land developer, real estate broker, or of some other associated profession, all play a major role in shaping our communities. Because of their varied backgrounds, they have diverse ideals of community planning. Therefore, so that each reader proceeds with a common perspective, a description of these professions is included.

## The Players

### LANDSCAPE ARCHITECTS

The landscape architect's role traditionally is recognized with regard to horti-cultural design. However, most of this professional's training is devoted to land-use planning. Site analysis and master planning are the true realm of landscape architecture. Professional requirements encourage the development of a broad perspective of service and involvement and provide a number of opportunities for their practice. Whether self-employed, a member of a design team in a landscape architectural, engineering, or architectural firm, or on the staff of a municipal, state, or federal agency, the landscape architect recog-nizes the ramifications of community in the larger context and therefore is positioned to play a key role in the planning process as liaison between the municipal planner and the land developer.

### CIVIL ENGINEERS

The civil engineer, whose training is preparatory to the task of infrastructure design and utility construction, ensures that the service requirements of the community with regard to roads, water, sewer, and power are adequately provided. As a consultant in the private sector, this professional not only provides construction documentation but may assist in the bidding and nego-tiation phases of contracts, and may serve as the client's agent during the municipal approval process. When employed by a municipal government, the civil engineer is given the responsibility of oversight by assuring that pro-posed development conforms to the established policy and procedural specifi-cations of the specific locality. With the emphasis on detail and construction cost control, an engineer may tend to lose sight of the true goal of the particu-lar project. In community planning terms, this goal must revolve around max-imizing the desirability and value of a product, not necessarily on producing it at the lowest cost.

### ARCHITECTS

The architect is traditionally the designer of buildings. However, this role also includes providing the focus necessary to coordinate and manage the complex process that transforms detailed drawings into the built environment. The architect most often uses site-planning techniques to maximize the impact of individual structures, thereby leaving to chance the larger issue of context. Although there are visionaries within this field who seek to solve the complex problems facing urbanized areas by exploring alternatives to tradi-tional community design, their impact is limited to a few select sites in a few select cities. The ideas presented here can assist the architect in introducing the developer to alternative approaches in site design that reduce the risk of repeating past mistakes.

## MUNICIPAL PLANNERS

The municipal planner's role includes the creation of policy and long-term goals for the public welfare. Options for master circulation routes and zoning and subdivision ordinances are studied in the development of comprehensive plans that guide the future growth of the municipality. As proposals for new construction are submitted by land developers, elected officials depend on the municipal planning director for guidance with regard to rezoning applications and proposed changes in current policy. Their daily activities tend to focus on the community impact of development proposals, and their long-range planning on the appropriateness of land uses for a particular area, which leaves them little time to graphically explore alternatives to typical site-design problems. It is our hope to provide realistic examples of quality physical planning.

## ELECTED OFFICIALS

Elected officials (such as members of the city council) very often have no training in a design or planning field and must depend on guidance from the municipal planning staff. Crucial issues with regard to the design of the community are often decided on the basis of political expediency rather than good planning criteria. Public opinion, swayed by special interest groups and magnified by the media, causes a reactionary response to issues relevant to growth, rather than a consideration of the long-term good of the community at large. Other civic groups, such as planning commissions and economic advisory boards, may be appointed to serve as consultants, but ultimately the elected official is accountable for the decisions made during his or her tenure. The examples offered here can assist in reducing the learning curve for the newly elected or appointed official and provide a refreshing update on newer planning solutions for the veteran.

## LAND DEVELOPERS

The land developer may be an individual, a group of businessmen, or a corporation whose role is to provide a product that the market will embrace. The ultimate goal is to introduce a needed element into the community at the highest potential return on the investment. The project must be performed within the system of growth outlined by the policies of a given municipality. Therefore the developer employs the expertise of professional designers and planners to provide various design scenarios for the land to be developed. It is the responsibility of these consultants to provide alternatives that are both buildable and feasible. If the determined best usage of the land does not conform to the municipality's existing comprehensive plan, an application for rezoning must be sought. By helping the land developers protect themselves against ill-advised design solutions offered by underinformed consultants, the solutions presented here can arm them with the knowledge to actively participate in the site-design process.

## REAL ESTATE BROKERS

Real estate brokers are involved in both the initial land acquisition phase and the product marketing phase once the development of a parcel of property has been approved by a municipality. Although they may be well versed in putting the deal together, they may not be as well informed on the difference between good design and poor design. In fact, they most likely depend on the shared, handed-down knowledge of those who preceded them. It is in this manner that misconceptions and mistakes are propagated. This book offers a short course in community design that can reduce the learning curve for new agents and retool the veteran.

There has been much debate as to the ideal solutions to the problems that face our expanding communities. In the chapters that follow we will explore the mechanism of community design from concept to implementation. We will identify the critical information that drives the design process and explore the creative inspiration that leads to practical solutions. Further, we will examine where we live, work, and relax, as well as where we spend our money. We will discuss the implications of putting it all together and keeping it together.

This book is meant to educate the reader in the process of community design. The theories that are found in it have been developed through years of professional practice. It is not our intent to dictate a philosophy, but to create a platform for understanding among colleagues. Use these pages to cooperate with each other as you effect positive changes in your own communities.

# CHAPTER 1

# So, What Is Community, Anyway?

It is safe to conclude that in the latter part of the twentieth century, we have forgotten how to plan communities. In city planning, we have been so preoccupied with parcel plan reviews that focus myopically on the minutiae of detail that we have either failed to recognize the product of this approach, or are powerless to prevent it within established criteria. Either way, we must reassess our current forms of habitable human space and begin to think of our communities as viable functioning forums of interaction. We must realize that communities need to grow consciously into a preconceived vision, rather than into an urban form created by mandated minimums.

Community has taken many forms throughout recorded history. Whether it is the wandering tribes of early man, the medieval concept of landschaft, the New England town and commons, the grid of small-town America, the urban core, or the suburbs, people's relationship with their environment and other people has fluctuated and adapted to change. The cities of the world that have weathered the test of time and remained vigorous population centers have evolved through hundreds, and in some cases, even thousands of years of constant modification. They have a reason for being, which has not been erroneously contrived but has responded and been adapted to the societal evolution of the centuries. Regardless of their founders' reasons for creating them, they have survived because they fulfill the commercial, social, and psychological needs of their citizens. The character and identity for which they are well known have developed as a direct response to their citizens' need for order and sense of place. The success of the great cities of the world is due in large part to the trial-and-error method of the forebearers of community and city planning as they refined the best components while discarding the unsuccessful, hapless ones that failed to serve their intended purpose. That which remains is not so much a testimony to the ingenuity of the planners, but rather reveals the present stage of the continuing evolutionary process of development.

Today, technology allows us to change the form of our cities and communities with such speed that the incremental changes that once occurred over the course of centuries now can be completed in only a matter decades. The patterns of growth that led to the development of such cities as Charleston, South Carolina, can be re-created, for good or ill, in a matter of just a few short years. As a case in point, Charleston has survived earthquakes, fires, hurricanes, wars, and economic upheaval, yet it endures as a livable city with much appeal for its citizens and the many tourists who visit every year. The allure of the historic district, with its crowded streets, shops, and gardens requires that community planners take a long look at a method of design that has long since been abandoned for more modern theories.

The development of the suburbs as a response to the mass exodus from the crowded conditions of the urban core embodied the principles of Ebenezer Howard's Garden City movement. Howard's optimum living environment consisted of the culture and services of the city, combined with the soothing environs of the trees and ponds of the countryside. Modern community planners interpret this ethic in terms of quality-of-life issues, livable space, sense of place, identity, and familiarity.

Contrast this with the development of Tyson's Corner, Virginia, one of the largest metropolitan areas in the United States. Originally a suburb of Washington, D.C., it is now a bustling commercial center for eight to ten

**Figure 1.1**   Charleston, South Carolina, streetscape.

**Figure 1.2**    Typical suburban development. (*Courtesy of CMSS Architects*)

hours a day, five days a week, and, with the exception of the high-rise condominiums and apartments, is primarily a sterile sequence of uninhabited spaces for the rest of the time. Commuter traffic jams during those rush hours at both dawn and sunset see people coming from and escaping to the more humane confines of familiarity and pedestrian scale. However, the consequences of this daily ritual have placed enormous stresses on the small outlying communities and residential suburbs. The resulting problems include overcrowding, increased costs of development, snarled highways, skyrocketing land costs, and increasing taxes, as well as steadily increasing costs for services and maintenance. All of these undercut the familiarity and scale that were the reason for moving "out" in the first place. The wisdom of the ages that continues to make Charleston a thriving walkable downtown community somehow escaped the attention of the planners of Tyson's Corner and of a myriad of other American cities and suburbs. The problem? We have too long mistaken *aggregation* for *community* and curb appeal for a sense of place.

## Community: What It Is and What It Isn't

*Community* has a variety of connotations, but, first, let's clear up a few misconceptions about it. Community is not a random accumulation of parts or sections loosely tied together by roads and waterways. Nor is it the homogeneous glut of interchangeable shopping centers, office buildings, housing, and open spaces that can be found without much effort in most American metropolitan areas. The result of this approach is that Orlando resembles Oshkosh, which resembles Oakland, which even resembles Ottawa, and the list goes on.

Community also must not be thought of as an alliance of special interest groups all clamoring for attention and demanding that their concerns be addressed. The divisiveness of this concept is the antithesis of community. According to *Merriam-Webster's Collegiate Dictionary,* Tenth Edition, community is "an interacting population of various kinds of individuals (as species) in a common location" or "a group of people with a common characteristic or interest living together within a larger society."[1] Additionally, it can mean the area in which a population lives, and may be identified with a way of life, such as a farming or fishing community, a steel town, or a college or university town. A community may be known for some specific trait such as innovation, ingenuity, determination, or traditional values and morality, as in the Amish communities of Pennsylvania. The term *community* also suggests a certain amount of interdependence and self-sufficiency, sometimes a result of necessity, as during the colonial period when settlers in the New World banded together for mutual protection and social support.

In their book *City Lights, An Introduction to Urban Studies,* E. Barbara Phillips and Richard T. LeGates argue that community has no agreed-upon meaning, but that it usually refers to (1) a group sharing a physical space, (2) a group sharing a common trait, or (3) a group bound together by shared identity and common culture and typified by a high degree of social cohesion.[2] If we were to use these definitions as criteria, most of the post-World War II–era suburbs would probably not pass the test.

In all fairness, however, most of these areas to some degree do exhibit the more limited qualities of neighborhood. Again, for our purposes here, let's quote Webster's. It defines neighborhood as "a section lived in by neighbors and usually having distinguishing characteristics."[3] Well, in our market-oriented society the term *distinguishing characteristics* has been reduced to *product type,* and *neighbors* to *target market.* Much like a centrifuge, the frenzied growth since the 1940s has served to separate and distill the various segments of society into increasingly thinner bands or cross sections of socioeconomically similar peoples into residential areas of practically indistinguishable housing. The result of this lack of order, organization, and sense of place is that community as we have defined it has in a large part been lost.

*Community,* as a concept, can be interpreted as a sense of belonging, a way of life, and diversity with a common purpose. In modern times, technology has made the compact community unnecessary in the purely physical sense, and our resultant mobility has eroded our spiritual and emotional connection to our civic places. This emotional disassociation has allowed us to raze, in a wholesale manner, entire sections of our cities and communities in the name of redevelopment; this has led to further psychic distress. All the while, we have been creating acres and acres of new housing and shopping centers blithely named Rolling Meadows Estates or Foxhound Forest or Avalon Acres.

In our rush to accommodate demographic lurches, we have substituted subdivision layout for community design and shopping center trips for social

[1]*By permission. From* Merriam-Webster's Collegiate® Dictionary, Tenth Edition. Copyright 1993 by Merriam-Webster Inc., publisher of the Merriam-Webster® dictionaries.

[2]E. Barbara Phillips and Richard T. LeGates. *City Lights, An Introduction to Urban Studies,* New York: Oxford University Press, 1981.

[3]*By permission. From* Merriam-Webster's Collegiate® Dictionary, Tenth Edition. Copyright 1993 by Merriam-Webster Inc., publisher of the Merriam-Webster® dictionaries.

interaction. In other words, we as community planners have been *reacting* to the frenzied pace of development, and not *managing* or *directing* it. To a large extent, the talent of community planning has atrophied through disuse. We must begin again to think of our communities in terms of human scale rather than automobile scale. Attention to the time-distance relationship between our housing, employment, shopping, and recreation areas is critical if we are to achieve any realistic sense of community. Our cities and communities need to be of a finer texture, allowing more opportunity for interaction among our diverse peoples and thus enhancing our understanding of one another by identifying and focusing on the commonalities among us. Community, therefore, is *belonging*; community is *a common purpose.*

Community planners need to interpret their heritage and learn to apply it to the task of creating and re-creating the communities of today. George Tobey, in his book *A History of Landscape Architecture: The Relationship of People to the Environment,* says that we need to establish goals that guide our planning efforts. He suggests that the values, habits, and objectives of the community's citizens must be addressed if *community* is to be achieved. From the physical standpoint, he suggests that good communities should adequately provide the means for moving goods, people, and information, and allow for the maximum freedom of choice in interaction among residents while providing for their health, safety, and comfort. He further states that good communities are adaptable to future modification, and their image be maintained as a unified whole.[4] To these, we may add goals that are tailored to our community's specific circumstances. The list is flexible and may change but the end result should be the same: a methodology of workable parameters from which to approach the healthy growth of our communities.

What's the next step? Putting our goals into action. To do this we need to inventory the physical design tools of our trade. These tools are the building blocks that will help us understand our task and enable us to comprehend the subtle nuances of community form.

## The Building Blocks

For the esoteric nature of community to be realized, practical forms must be given to it. From a physical standpoint, the incremental elements apparent in successful communities can be inferred from Kevin Lynch's views in *The Image of the City.* To Lynch, paths, edges, districts, nodes, and landmarks are the elements that give form to cities by evoking an image that is recognized, be it consciously or subconsciously.[5]

[4]George B. Tobey. *A History of Landscape Architecture: The Relationship of People to the Environment,* originally published by the American Elsevier Publishing Company, Inc., and now distributed by Books on Demand, a division of University Microfilms International, Ann Arbor, Mich., 1973.

[5]Kevin Lynch. *The Image of the City,* Cambridge, Mass.: M.I.T. Press, 1960.

## PATHS

Paths or channels of movement are the predominant form-giving element within a city; these include streets, walkways, transit lines, canals, railroads, and interstate highways. They are the lifelines along which most activity takes place and adjacent to which lie all the functions on which a city depends: government, industry, commerce, and housing. They can reinforce an image of order and unity or, in worst-case scenarios, exacerbate chaos.

## EDGES

Edges are linear elements not used or considered as paths; they are the boundaries between different kinds of districts. While not as dominant as paths, they are interpreted as strong organizing elements. A waterfront, a mountain range, and the boundary between a floodplain and higher ground are all strong edges. They can be solid and impenetrable, resulting in abrupt differences from one side to the other such as an edge of a marsh, or they can be diffused and unfocused as in the edge created by the limits of the urban services boundary of a community (i.e., sanitary sewer lines, water mains, etc.).

**Figure 1.3**  A garden path.

**Figure 1.4**  A suburban path. (*Courtesy of CMSS Architects*)

**Figure 1.5**  A river front as an edge. (*Courtesy of CMSS Architects*)

DISTRICTS

Districts are areas that can consciously be entered. Buildings or structures within a district share certain commonalities and characteristics that can be recognized. Greenwich Village of New York City, the Mission District of San Francisco, and the French Quarter of New Orleans all exhibit separate and distinct scale, texture, and structural elements to the degree that they are easily perceived as a place. People use districts to help them mentally organize the layout of a community and to aid in reducing an area of overwhelming scale to one that can be more easily managed. Districts exhibit a certain theme or visual clarity that evokes a distinct identity. A waterfront warehousing area, a downtown financial center, or a gentrified upscale housing zone each has a distinct scale, texture, and use.

NODES

Nodes are specific points in a city that have name or place recognition value. They are points to and from which people travel, and very often they serve as the center or core of a district. To Lynch, nodes are closely associated with paths and thus can also be found at the transition points between districts. Picadilly Circus, Times Square, and the Grand Mall in Washington, D.C., are all junctions of paths and exhibit the characteristics of nodes. Another important characteristic of nodes is that they usually are thematic in nature. Clusters of like uses tend to result in a discernible sense of association. Again, Times Square and 42nd Street in New York for their theaters, the Grand Mall in Washington, D.C., for its government buildings and museums, and almost any seaside resort for its tee shirt shops.

LANDMARKS

Landmarks are very similar to nodes but usually are perceived as a single element, either structural or natural. They are the reference points used by all in navigating a path through the city and usually take the form of great public spaces, artwork, or significant buildings. Landmarks usually contrast greatly with the background in which they are perceived, which enhances their visual

**Figure 1.6**   The old Exchange Building in the Charleston, South Carolina, historic district is a prominent node.

**Figure 1.7**   A focal point provides a directional reference.

importance in the landscape as beacons or reference points. They evoke a feeling of familiarity with a particular area and help to establish an identity for it. The Eiffel Tower in Paris, the Gateway Arch of St. Louis, and Telegraph Hill of San Francisco are all fine examples of landmarks.

Although Lynch spoke of these elements as the building blocks of cities, we feel that they are universal and relevant at the community scale as well. In other words, good communities, like good cities, will possess the same physical elements; indeed, whole nations or regions of the earth can be thought of in this manner. It is easy to see how the Mississippi River, the Blue Ridge Mountains, the Great Plains, the city of Chicago, and Yosemite National Park exhibit the qualities of path, edge, district, node, and landmark, respectively, but at a much larger scale. The major difference between this national scale and the community scale is that in the former, these physical elements have more or less evolved, with people merely playing a role in their evolution. At the smaller community scale, the human race, as designer, becomes the active agent for change, using the concepts of paths, edges, districts, nodes, and landmarks as tools.

In the past, these five basic elements were used through trial and error to create the memorable human places of habitation throughout the world.

Change occurred slowly, almost imperceptibly during the life span of the average person. Good city and community design was rewarded with active use, embellishment, and longevity, while poor examples were reworked, eliminated, or abandoned. What has remained is a cumulative history of the best parts of city and community design.

## Tools of the Trade

Now that we have identified the elements of community, how can we combine or organize them to create better communities? First, we must recognize that they are the methods through which viewers define and orient themselves within a given space. Also, we must be cognizant that a well-designed space or, for that matter, a community, by definition must exhibit the same principles of design that any true work of art exhibits: primarily harmony, gradation, contrast, and unity. While all successful works of fine art maintain these principles, they are created by artists who use the elements of line, direction, shape, size, texture, value, and color to organize their canvas into a perceptible image. In the same way, the community planner uses a distinct but dissimilar palette of spatial organizing elements, which include axial design, hierarchical systems, transition elements, dominant features, and a sense of enclosure to create a successful community.

AXIAL DESIGN
Axial design is a strongly visual and very powerful space articulator and usually tends to overpower the other organizing elements. It is linear in nature, is used to establish order, and serves to connect two or more features or terminal points. While the concept of axial design is more closely associated with formality and rigidity, it can be used in more subtle ways to create curving vistas that direct one's view to a series of terminal points.

One of the best examples of formal axial design is the town plan of Colonial Williamsburg. With the capitol building at one end and the College of William and Mary at the other end of Duke of Gloucester Street, shops, offices, and homes form the background of a very powerful relationship in spatial design. Whether it is used in a formal, symmetrical way or in an informal, asymmetrical one, axial design must successfully employ movement, function, and visual perception.

HIERARCHY
Hierarchy, or gradation of design features, plays an important role in any spatial design. Utilizing a variety of sizes of spaces or *outdoor rooms* not only creates variety in the landscape, but helps the designer to clearly delineate the more important "rooms" from the minor, support areas. Effective use of gradation is one of the best methods one can employ in reducing a grandly scaled space to a more comfortable human scale, and vice versa. Drama and excitement can be enhanced greatly with careful attention to hierarchical design.

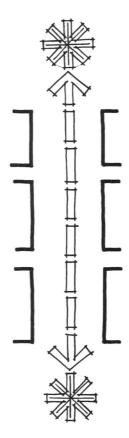

**Sketch 1.1**  Axial design.

**Figure 1.8**  Versailles is a good example of axial design. (*Photo taken by Robert McDuffie*)

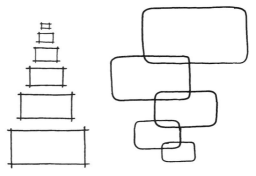

**Sketch 1.2**   Hierarchy/gradation.

## TRANSITION ELEMENTS

Exterior spaces can be seemingly endless and filled with a tremendous variety of objects, structures, and landscapes. However, they can be softened or blended by the use of *transition elements*. These elements are necessary if the space is to be considered complete or coherent. Because humans must be able to organize their environment to function in it effectively, the arrangement of the visual field is crucial to wayfinding and a sense of place. Transitions are overlap areas that exhibit characteristics of both or all of the spaces that meet in a certain location. Repetition of a design element, similar sizing, coloring of architectural features or landscape material, even the continuation of a paving pattern are all examples of transitional elements.

## DOMINANT FEATURES

Just as music crescendos to a climax and art needs a focus, outdoor spaces and communities are more effective and complete if a dominant element is discernible. This focal point gives a place a purpose; otherwise, the space is

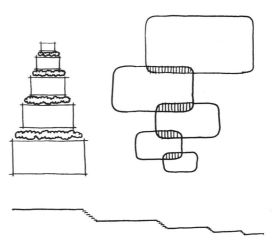

**Sketch 1.3**   Transition.

empty and unfulfilled. A focal point not only gives a space a "reason" for existing, but in so doing creates unity within the space. The dominant feature of a space or community completes the picture or creates a sense of the whole. However, too many dominant features within a given area create too many elements vying for attention, which results in confusion. The single church spire of a medieval village, the way a baseball stadium is built around home plate, and the statuary or fountain feature usually found in civic spaces, create a center which all other elements of the space support.

SENSE OF ENCLOSURE

Creating a sense of enclosure is perhaps the single most important feature in the design of community spaces. Formed by the careful manipulation of the ground plane, the overhead plane, and the vertical or wall plane, enclosure can be created to fit the use or activity desired, and thus establish the scale of the space. The activities or emotions that result from a walk down a friendly main street, a quiet conversation in an intimate town house garden, or a coin toss at the 50-yard line of a 10,000-seat stadium are all quite different, but yet are all at home in their respective spaces.

In the same way, there is a direct relationship between the height of the vertical elements and the horizontal distance between them that must be

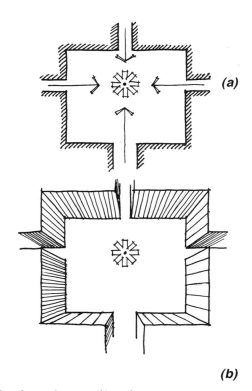

Sketch 1.4   (a) Dominant element; (b) enclosure.

**Figure 1.9** A stadium provides another kind of enclosure.

respected in creating a functional yet comfortable space. When the height of the verticals is greater than the distance between them, one becomes more aware of the vertical elements themselves rather than the space they create. If the distance between the vertical elements exceeds four times their height, then the sense of enclosure is lost altogether. The most comfortable community spaces are those that fall between these two extremes at a ratio of two or three horizontal units to one vertical unit. With this ratio in mind, we can easily understand why shopping center parking lots and wide suburban parkways with extended building setback lines seem empty and undesirable, lacking richness of scale and texture.

## Spatial Components

Circulation, open space, and structures are the primary aspects of spatial design, and are manipulated by the designer to create ordered, contextual, and unique realms for human activity. No matter what the scale, the design process consists of the conscious arranging and rearranging of these three elements in the two-dimensional plane for three-dimensional application.

**Figure 1.10** A suburban intersection provides little, if any, enclosure.

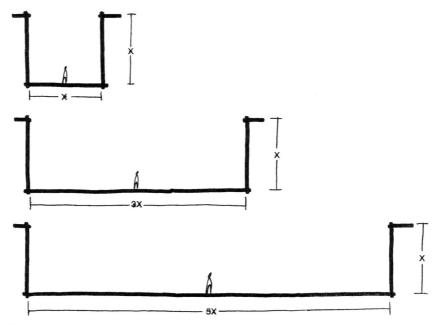

**Sketch 1.5** Enclosure ratios.

## CIRCULATION

Circulation systems allow movement and mobility, enriching a static space, making it alive and fluid with ever-changing experiences. However, overemphasis of this spatial use of circulation can eliminate the diversity on which good, functional spaces rely. The almost inevitable growth of the two-lane farm roads into six- and eight-lane commuter collector streets is an example of the overemphasis on function at the expense of perceived space. It is also easy to understand how this overemphasis has resulted in our suburban environments evolving into single-use sites or districts.

## OPEN SPACE

Open space, the seemingly void zone between vertical elements, can be perceived as being positive, productive, planned, and functionally supportive, or as negative, wasted, unstructured, and deleterious. Too often in our suburban areas, open space merely is that area left over by mandated minimum setbacks and conveniently placed buffer areas between incompatible uses. More often than not this effort is a mere ploy to gain the approval of some regulatory authority.

In community design, open space must be thought of as the most ethereal of the fundamental building blocks in quality design. It should never be considered as an afterthought or just as the leftovers. If the viewer can perceive open space as a part of a larger composition, one that heightens the relationship of the other elements in that composition, then that space has been successfully designed.

## STRUCTURES

Structures, the manufactured forms in which we live, work, shop, and play are the destinations of our daily activities. They can either be harmonious and contextual or discordant and contrary. Open space, like water, is fluid and tends to escape unless held in place by strong elements and structures. Richly detailed architecture that strives to break down larger building walls into more human-scaled projections and indentations create texture, and is therefore more successful at "holding" space than are monochromatic, slick, single-plane walls. Interest, in the form of shadows, reveal lines, and tactile surfaces, must be designed into walls if people are to comfortably use and relate to the spaces they surround. As we have seen, the height of buildings with respect to the associated open space is pivotal in reinforcing a sense of enclosure. Likewise, the quality of an open space is further reinforced if the

**Figure 1.11**  Human-scaled architecture.

**Figure 1.12**  Inhuman-scaled architecture.

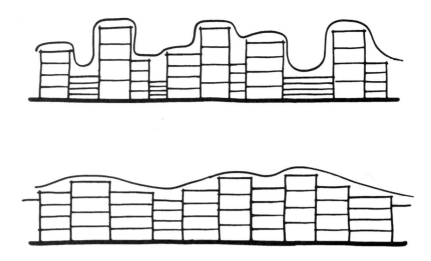

**Sketch 1.6** Adjacent building heights shouldn't vary by more than 25 percent of the smaller building.

heights of the buildings enclosing it do not vary by more than 25 percent. However, unless the space is enclosed with a single building of uniform height, multiple buildings of exactly uniform height should also be avoided in order to ensure variety and interest through shadows and reveal lines. This type of building articulation also helps people to reference their progress through a space. Merely projecting in the mind's eye the edges of buildings into the space, makes it easy to approximate one's position and in so doing reduces its volume to human scale.

## In Summary

Lynch's paths, edges, districts, nodes, and landmarks used in combination with the concepts of axial design, hierarchical systems, transition elements, dominant features, and enclosure are the building blocks and tools we need to create communities that are livable and dynamic. What we have described is classic urban design, which should be applied to the community scale. A basic understanding of the ingredients necessary for successful community design must include forms and patterns that are flexible with regard to the common goals of the citizenry. Any prevalent theme or special characteristic that enhances the common heritage and familiarity promoted by the pedestrian scale will help to build an innovative network of environmental, cultural, and social systems that establishes context and rhythm while avoiding monotonous repetition.

# CHAPTER 2

# Groundwork: Where Do I Begin?

The process of community planning cannot be undertaken without a rudimentary understanding of the complexity that results when humans decide to live among one another. In order to effectively use the building blocks of community, we must understand the context in which we will work. In the United States, various types of information exist that give community planners vital clues to the interaction of people with each other as well as with their environment. Ideally, this information constitutes a tangible record of the cause and effect between humans and nature, but more simply it is a catalog of our actions. It identifies what we know about ourselves and our environment as well as the changes we have made and the constraints we impose on ourselves in order to protect both. As community planners it is our responsibility to analyze as many pertinent sources of information as possible to understand the impact of changes we might propose, as well as to evaluate the consequences of our past decisions. Only when we thoroughly review all pertinent information are we ready to effect any new changes to our communities.

## What Kind of Information Should Be Considered and Where Do I Find It?

There is a vast amount of information available through federal, state, and local government agencies as well as local planning district commission offices. By highlighting the sources that follow we don't mean to imply that they are the only ones you'll ever need, but they are a great place to start. Obviously, the issues of most importance in your community will vary somewhat from your colleagues' and what you need in the way of background data may be unique. For instance, communities surrounding the Chesapeake Bay or located along its tributaries will be affected by the regulations of the Chesapeake Bay Preservation Act. Municipalities in environmentally sensitive areas may have more complete comprehensive growth management plans than those for whom uncontrolled growth is not an issue.

The scale of a project will be the deciding factor as to the kinds of information you will want to seek out. For example, it is unlikely that you would need to consult a federal agency for regional economic indicators when you are considering the development of a 30,000-square foot office building or a small commercial site. Nor would it be responsible to propose a mixed-use housing development without considering the availability of adequate sewer and water service. As we discuss the types of data and their sources, remember that their names may vary throughout the country, but the type of information is typical of what you can find with a little effort.

## Municipal Governments

The municipal government is a primary source of pertinent community information. The types of data that can be obtained are comprehensive growth studies and zoning, site plan, and subdivision ordinances, which include such agenda as the landscape ordinance, zoning maps, tax and topographic maps, planimetrics, sewer and water service maps, master street and highway maps, bikeway maps, and the list goes on. Copies of these sources can be either purchased or reviewed in the offices of planning or engineering services, and they come in a variety of scales from 1" = 100' to 1" = 2000'. The maps are useful for creating accurate base sheets for design development and presentations to clients and public bodies. This also expedites the graphic representation of ideas that will be translated into detailed construction drawings.

### Comprehensive Growth Studies

Urban sprawl, or uncontrolled development, is a heated political issue for many municipalities. Growth, when left to happen piecemeal, can consume valuable land resources and destroy irreplaceable natural treasures. Many cities and towns have found it necessary to establish a formal statement of development and planning policy. Ideally, it should outline a comprehensive strategy for growth that preserves valuable land reserves while helping to foster optimum economic viability. It may address long- and short-term goals and explore future challenges while providing a platform for amendments to accommodate changes in technology and refinements in planning theory.

In order to simplify the task, the plan may break down the city into planning zones. Land-use acreage tabulations may be included for each zone with regard to single-family and multi-family units, commercial and industrial space, open space, and so on, and whether these are over or under target projections. The issues most commonly discussed include existing and proposed housing, transportation networks, environmental conservation areas, and public facilities, which include existing and future schools, fire and police stations, libraries, parks and recreation facilities, sewer and water services, bikeways, as well as overall drainage considerations, economic development target areas, and objectives.

Some of the more extensive comprehensive plans provide design guidelines for preferred ways of developing these ideas. Loudon County, Virginia, is a good example of this. Others only state policies and objectives, and stop woefully short of creating a framework for action. Whichever type you may have, the municipality's *Comprehensive Plan* is required reading for all who are contemplating land development or are in any way involved in the growth industry.

## Zoning Ordinances

Zoning can be defined as the classification of land-use types that establishes a range of possible development options for a piece of property. Simply stated, it establishes what can and cannot occur on a given property. These land uses are identified in the zoning ordinance of a municipality and deal with land use on the basis of intensity. The various types include but are not necessarily limited to office, commercial, agricultural, residential, industrial, conservation, recreational, resort, and historic preservation. The goal of zoning is to ensure the compatibility of adjacent land uses and reduce conflicts between land-use types. Within each land-use category, a range of factors with a graduated scale of use intensity is stipulated with regard to allowable conditions and specifications. For example, the uses outlined in the residential category range from high-density multi-family units to single-family detached dwellings on large lots. Each category includes a set of regulations defining minimum standards for layout, setback from the public right-of-way, allowable density in units per acre, parking space requirements, maximum building square footage, and so forth. The compatibility of any proposed changes to the community must follow the guidelines of the zoning ordinance and meet all relevant criteria.

## Zoning Maps

Zoning maps show how land within the community has been classified with regard to the regulations of the zoning code. Zoning maps usually are drawn at a scale of 1" = 200' or 1" = 400' and can be obtained from the municipal

**Figure 2.1** Portion of a zoning map. (*Courtesy of the City of Virginia Beach*)

planning department. During the initial stages of research, zoning maps are helpful in pinpointing appropriately sized parcels for an intended land use, as well as determining which parcels could be considered for a change of zoning classification to allow a different and more intense use. This element of land development will be discussed further later.

### Subdivision Ordinances

The subdivision ordinance establishes regulations that govern how parcels of land are subdivided and developed. While it may include the procedure for the transfer of property titles, as a rule it will not deal with the actual placement of buildings on the lot. This is reserved for the site plan ordinance.

Meeting the requirements of the subdivision ordinance requires the development of preliminary and final subdivision plats, which are prepared to ensure that all required improvements are achieved with regard to street width and road location as per a municipality's master street and highway plan. Detailed specifications for streets and street signage, street lights, traffic control devices, sidewalks, alleys, driveway entrances, lot sizes, setbacks, easements, public sites, and recreation areas, and so on, are established to ensure that a uniform system is maintained. Also included are the rules for seeking a variance to any of the requirements in cases where meeting specific criteria may place undue hardship or burden on the property owner. More importantly, this procedure is an opportunity for imaginative designers to circumvent the standardized mandates in order to introduce a better product.

## Site Plan Ordinances

The site plan ordinance is the set of guidelines that must be adhered to in order to obtain a building permit. It relates directly to the zoning ordinance in that it establishes the construction specifications, i.e., length, width, and minimum and maximum square footage for such things as parking spaces, lot coverage, stormwater management areas, drainage structure, street and curb details, landscape requirements, and so on.

## Topographic Maps

Generalized topographic information produced at a scale of 1" = 2000' can be obtained from maps created by the United States Geological Survey and will be discussed later. However, many communities have created comprehensive topographic maps at a scale of 1" = 100' which can be found at the municipal surveyor's office. The contour interval may vary depending on the terrain, but will usually be between 1 and 5 feet and should identify all major high and low points as spot elevations. Topographic maps are useful because they provide a basis for preliminary engineering and feasibility analysis during the initial stages of planning. They provide the community planner with an accurate source of topographic data without incurring the expense of a full-scale physical survey. They can be counted on for accuracy to within plus or minus 5 percent. However, this information should not be substituted for a complete site survey prior to the development of construction documents.

## Planimetrics

Planimetrics show the accurate placement of lot lines and such physical features as trees, buildings, roads, ditch lines, and so forth. They are usually at a scale of 1" = 100' and can be obtained in the survey and mapping department of a municipality or at the city or county engineer's office. While they do not necessarily show vertical topographic information, they are useful because they provide an accurate representation of the physical objects occurring in the landscape. Obviously, the more recent the map, the more current the information. However, older planimetrics are also helpful in gaining an insight into the past uses of a property and in determining the original lay of the land and its drainage patterns. Planimetrics can be used in conjunction with tax, zoning, and topographic maps to provide some initial impressions of a site.

## Tax Maps

Tax maps show the lot boundaries and their approximate area in acres, fractions thereof, or square feet. They also include the name of the owner and the estimated value of the property. Tax maps can be obtained from the city assessor's office, and allow the community planner to identify current land uses and begin to determine future trends for the area as well as whether a property is over- or undervalued. Tax maps also serve as a means to verify information gleaned from the planimetrics. In smaller municipalities, tax maps may be freehand drawn, very obtuse, and not to be trusted as a reliable source of basesheet information. However, more municipalities are having them professionally produced to scale, and these are therefore as reliable as planimetrics. In any case, it is always a good idea to consult more than one source of information to ferret out any inconsistencies. Accuracy in base information is crucial to successful community design. However, surprises can and do occur, so it is wise to be as thorough as possible.

## Sanitary Sewer Maps

Sanitary sewer maps are a necessary source of information when contemplating infrastructure requirements for proposed growth. Their accuracy is limited, as they are a diagrammatic representation only of the overall layout of this utility. They can be obtained at the city engineer's office or public utilities department and show major trunk lines, gravity interceptors, and sanitary sewer force mains on maps at scales between 1" = 1200' and 1" = 1800'. Individual sewer lines, manholes, and rim and invert elevations are shown on maps of 1" = 200' to 1" = 400'. When used in conjunction with zoning and topographic maps, they provide a general understanding of the direction of flow, current capacity, and how far or whether a line can be extended. Service taps are made into a four- or eight-inch pipe that allows the waste water to flow by gravity to increasingly larger lines collecting from a greater and greater area. Unless they flow directly to a treatment facility, they terminate in a pumping station where the wastewater is gathered and pushed to a treatment facility. For those who can decipher them, calculations concerning existing pumping station capacities can be obtained from the municipal engineer's office. When the goal is to extend service into new areas, it is usually wise for the designer types to defer sewer system design to a qualified engineer who specializes in infrastructure. He or she can advise as to what, if any, modifications can be made to increase capacity. This information is useful when discussing the impact of growth as well as doing long-range projections for future service needs.

## Water Service Maps

Water maps are usually drawn to the same scale as sanitary sewer maps and generally can be obtained from the same sources. They show the location and size of all water lines, valves, and fire hydrants. Calculations as to the amount

**Figure 2.2** A water main map. (*Courtesy of the City of Virginia Beach*)

of pressure available in each area can be obtained from the city engineer's office or the municipal water authority. Water maps are useful because they help to determine the availability of water and the cost of providing it to a site, and they provide crucial information with regard to project feasibility.

## Local Regulatory Guidelines

Local regulatory guidelines usually are established within the context of special circumstances. Many municipalities have developed regulations to maintain the integrity of historic districts, to protect environmentally sensitive areas, or to limit the impact of or to prevent inevitable conflicts between certain land uses. Cities such as Charleston, South Carolina, Savannah, Georgia, and Williamsburg, Virginia, to name a few, have designated historic districts that are maintained by strict architectural guidelines. Design review committees must approve proposed changes or improvements prior to the issuance of building permits.

In other cases, municipalities are required to respect national guidelines in order to protect valuable resources that are shared by more than one state. As an example, the Chesapeake Bay Preservation Act affects communities in the Chesapeake Bay watershed by limiting encroachment on its tidal wetlands and tributaries and seeking to reduce and ultimately eliminate sources of pollution (see Sketch 2.1). Some states have their own preservation areas, for which strict limitations on growth have been implemented; the most comprehensive is New Jersey's Pinelands Preservation Area. Many communities have established master street and highway plans, and bikeway and greenway plans. Streets and highways plans use codes and legends to categorize streets by the number of lanes, the presence of medians for divided and undivided boulevards, the recognition of scenic easements, and so forth. Bikeway plans show the network of paved surfaces designated as bikeways. This does not necessarily mean that the bikeway is a separate entity from a street or sidewalk but only that it exists, on paper at least, as part of a communitywide system.

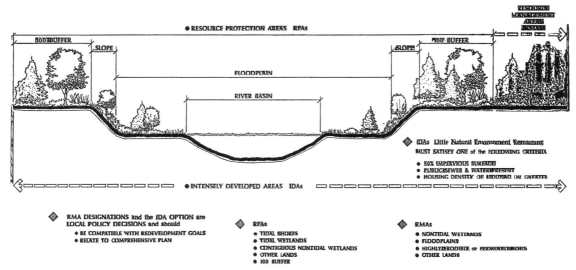

Within the sketch, the following labels appear:

● RESOURCE PROTECTION AREAS RPAs

RESOURCE MANAGEMENT AREAS RMAs

100' BUFFER   SLOPE   FLOODPLAIN   RIVER BASIN   SLOPE   100' BUFFER

IDAs Little Natural Environment Remaining
MUST SATISFY ONE of the FOLLOWING CRITERIA
● 50% IMPERVIOUS SURFACE
● PUBLIC SEWER & WATER PRESENT
● HOUSING DENSITY of 8 DU/AC or GREATER

● INTENSELY DEVELOPED AREAS IDAs

◆ RMA DESIGNATIONS and the IDA OPTION are LOCAL POLICY DECISIONS and should
● BE COMPATIBLE WITH REDEVELOPMENT GOALS
● RELATE TO COMPREHENSIVE PLAN

◆ RPAs
● TIDAL SHORES
● TIDAL WETLANDS
● CONTIGUOUS NONTIDAL WETLANDS
● OTHER LANDS
● 100 BUFFER

◆ RMAs
● NONTIDAL WETLANDS
● FLOODPLAINS
● HIGHLY ERODIBLE or PERMEABLE SOILS
● OTHER LANDS

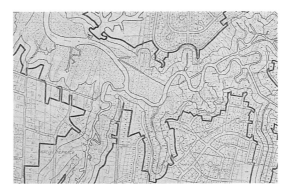

**Figure 2.3** Chesapeake Bay watershed map.

More and more municipalities are combining open-space preservation with the desire for greenway corridors in an effort to retain unique ecosystems while providing opportunities for recreation. Cities like Raleigh, North Carolina, are establishing extensive greenway systems that link several preservation areas, maximizing their usefulness as productive ecosystems and recreational amenities. Guidelines established to respect the integrity of bikeways and greenways must be reviewed in order to maximize the opportunities they provide.

## Regional Planning Agencies

An excellent source of all things demographic, regional planning agencies have a wide variety of books, maps, and aerial photographs that can be purchased. Whether you are creating your own reference library or you want information relevant to specific projects, this is one of your best sources. Planning district commissions, as they are sometimes called, provide a wealth of data on economic growth trends, as well as forecasts and inventories of human service resources. They also provide information pertaining to comprehensive management studies for physical and environmental planning as well as transportation. The information is not limited to regional specifics but is compared to national trends with regard to economic growth and legislative initiatives. Studies are published on a variety of topics such as housing for the elderly, poverty, watershed analysis, water quality, solid waste disposal, energy resource management, hazardous wastes, and scenic and open-space opportunities, to name a few. They provide an invaluable service by gathering and analyzing the data that would be too time-consuming and too tedious for community planners to do for themselves. You can find out if your area has a planning district commission by calling your municipal planning office.

## State Agencies

### State Highway Standards

Roads given the designation of state highways are owned by the state. Heretofore, they have been improved and maintained by the state department of transportation, with most of the mileage of these roads being in rural areas. However, as towns and cities have expanded, these roads have remained subject to the standards established by that state's highway department. Design requirements for speed, width, allowable frequency of intersections, curvature and radii, maximum superelevation and vertical curve, design specifications for bridges, culverts, cul-de-sacs, pavement composition, and so on, are provided in a publication that can be obtained from the state department of transportation.

## Federal Government Agencies

A myriad of information can be obtained from the various agencies and departments of the federal government. It is not our intent to list it all here, but you can be sure that there is an enormous amount of paper produced each year with regard to research and regulatory data. Each reader will have to determine what sources of information are essential to the task. You can easily be overwhelmed by what is available, but with a little forethought you can determine exactly what you need. The sources that follow are a proper beginning. If you find that you want or need more information, you can begin your search by telephoning the agencies that created the information we list.

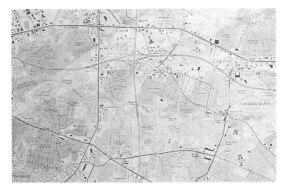

**Figure 2.4**  USGS topographic map.

## *USGS Maps*

The United States Geographical Information System produces 7.5 minute quadrangle maps at a scale of 1" = 2000'. Technically speaking, they are a polyconic projection subdivided at 10,000' grid ticks based on each state's coordinate system (longitude and latitude). They can be obtained from a U.S. Geological Survey office but may be found locally at technical supply stores that cater to engineering firms. In mountainous areas, USGS maps for that area may be carried by merchants who sell hiking and canoeing goods. The information is standardized to include generalized topography at 5- to 25-foot contour intervals, water bodies and their depth, streams and marsh areas, cleared and wooded areas, primary and secondary highways, and light duty and unimproved roads, as well as the general locations of buildings and cemeteries. USGS maps are useful as basesheets for large-scale conceptual planning. As a contextual source of information they provide a plethora of physical data that help community planners to maximize their research efforts.

## *U.S. Army Corps of Engineers*

The primary mission of the Corps is to provide planning, design, and construction services for the military, whether in war or peace. However, as directed by Congress, the Corps also has a rather extensive civil works program. Its responsibilities include:

- Administration of federal laws regulating the use of navigable waters; granting permits for the discharge of dredged or fill materials into those waters as mandated by the U.S. Clean Water Act
- Wetlands delineation and local assistance with compliance
- Comprehensive planning for river basin development
- Improvement of rivers for navigation; creation and protection of harbors

- Floodplain management, to include correction of drainage problems and flood control measures
- Beach erosion control and hurricane protection
- Damage control and rehabilitation assistance during natural disasters
- Assistance to local governments in regulating floodplains
- Regional water resource planning
- Regional wastewater management planning.[6]

*National Wetland Inventory (NWI) Maps*

The destruction of wetlands has been a source of much controversy. Subsequent regulatory legislation has attempted to classify wetlands according to productivity with regard to water quality for wildlife habitat and groundwater recharge. The information provided by National Wetland Inventory maps classifies wetland areas by ecological system, ecological subsystem, class, and subclass. Which system or type is considered to be useful wetlands according to regulatory criteria is the source of continuing debate. NWI maps are produced by the U.S. Fish and Wildlife Service and can be obtained from that source or, as with USGS maps, possibly from technical supply stores that cater to the needs of engineering firms. The maps may also be available through your regional planning commission offices or the local office of the U.S. Army Corps of Engineers. These maps identify

**Figure 2.5**    National Wetlands Inventory (NWI) map.

[6]U.S. Army Corps of Engineers.

the general location and type of wetlands within the quadrangle window of the USGS maps, at a scale of 1" = 2000'. This is a great advantage as it allows the two to be overlaid, thereby providing a source of base information for large-scale planning efforts. NWI maps are useful in that they provide a generalized inventory of possible wetland areas. However, detailed wetland analysis confirming the presence of wetlands must be done on a site-by-site basis by a qualified wetland scientist, and verified by the U.S. Army Corp of Engineers.

### Aerial Photographs

Aerial photographs help the community planner to identify natural and manufactured features for the interpretation, evaluation, and analysis of land resources. The level of accuracy required in the interpretation of existing conditions prior to land use planning necessitates a vigorous inventory of site characteristics. While site visits are strongly recommended, aerial photographs allow the site to be seen in context with its surroundings. Also, site characteristics that may be inadvertently overlooked during a site survey will be faithfully recorded on film.

There are a variety of sources for aerial photographs. The federal clearing house for high altitude and satellite photography is the Earth Resources Observation Systems (EROS) Data Center in Sioux Falls, South Dakota, which is managed by the U.S. Geological Survey. The EROS center's holdings contain some eight million frames, gathered from 1940 to the present, and include photographs obtained from the National Aeronautics and Space Administration (NASA), the National High Altitude Photography Program (NHAP, 1980–1987), and the National Aerial Photography Program (NAPP, 1987–1991). Both NHAP and NAPP were supported by a number of federal and state agencies including the Departments of Agriculture, Defense, and the Interior, and provide systematic coverage of the 48 conterminous United States. Strict flight parameters ensure minimum shadow and haze and no cloud cover.

The products available from the EROS center include black and white, natural color, and color infrared photographs; film transparencies, 35mm slides, and some digital scanner data. The photographs are taken in stereo pairs—two overlapping high-resolution, stereoscopic photographs—which can be viewed three dimensionally using a stereoscope.

The photographs are available in 9 × 9-inch contact prints, as well as (2×) 18 × 18, (3×) 27 × 27, (4×) 36 × 36-inch enlargements, and 35mm slides. You can also order special print sizes. EROS provides a free comprehensive index on microfiche, which provides all the information you need to order. One helpful hint: identify the map coordinates (longitude and latitude) of the area for which you want photographs on a USGS topographic map. This will be helpful when ordering. For further information you can contact the

**Figure 2.6**　High altitude, color infrared photo.

U.S. Geological Survey at the EROS Data Center in Sioux Falls, South Dakota 57198.

There are other sources of aerial photography; however, they may not be available in the scale you might want, the product you need (35mm slides, for instance), or might not be as current as the USGS products. Local offices of the U.S. Soil Conservation Service have black and white aerial photographs of the regions they serve, and these can be reviewed in their offices. You might also check the yellow pages of the telephone book. There may be aerial photography services that will take the pictures you need. It usually requires that you meet with the pilot/photographer to discuss the location and scale of the product you need. But don't forget to ask if there is an existing photograph of what you want; there's no use paying for extra flight time if you can get a copy of an existing photograph.

Another source is the state highway department, which uses aerial photographs for transportation analysis and planning. Again, you are limited to the scale they provide but most often they have up-to-date, reliable data.

And don't forget to ask if your municipality has aerial photographs. Some do, but the information may be limited and not recently flown. Older photographs can be useful, though, when you are trying to analyze growth or verify land-use patterns within your community. Land that has been left in its natural state for a decade or longer may have some development constraints that have been overlooked. However, you're probably going to be limited to viewing these photographs on the premises, but you might luck out; some cities have a complete set of aerials on mylar from which a blueprint can be made and purchased.

**Figure 2.7** Soils map.

### Soil Surveys

Soil surveys are published for each state by the U.S. Soil Conservation Service. These surveys discuss soil description, physiography, relief, drainage, and issues relevant to the use and management of soils. They provide detailed guidelines as to how land can and should be used with regard to crops and pasture, beaches and dunes, marsh and woodland management, recreation, and wildlife habitats. Soil types and their properties are listed, including freeze dates, growing season, capability, and projected yields of crops and pastureland, as well as the possibility of commercial application for forest products. Within the pages of the soil survey are maps at a scale of 1" = ¼ mile. The soils information is superimposed on an aerial photograph and identified by an abbreviation of the soil name.

The soil survey is a useful tool, because it provides a broad outline for land use by suggesting land-use possibilities with regard to soil type. The parameters for development recommended by the soil survey can influence recommendations by allowing the community planner to compare the cost of development of alternative sites based on soil permeability, depth, salinity, and shrink-swell potential and with regard to the soil amendments necessary to accommodate land uses that are not recommended. For more conclusive results, soil borings will be necessary to confirm the exact conditions of each site.

### AICUZ Maps

Air Installation Compatible Use Zones (AICUZ) maps diagram noise and accident potential (crash) zones in and around military airfields. They were developed by the Department of Defense in response to growing pressures for the development of land adjacent to military airfields. The zones coincide with the orbital air space and that used for landing approach and takeoff. Each zone is categorized on the basis of noise intensity and crash potential.

Compatible land uses are suggested to provide guidelines for surrounding development and to eliminate possible conflicts.

Civil airports have similar maps identifying high noise potential. A copy of one can be obtained from the airport manager's office or a local real estate association. And by the way, civil airport managers don't like to think of their maps as identifying crash potential. That makes them nervous. So humor them and be sure not to mention the "C" word.

*Floodplain Maps*

Many cities are located along waterways and in coastal regions. For construction within the floodplain, regulations are necessary in order to protect the integrity of the floodplain itself and to prevent, as much as humanly possible, the likelihood of floods that result in collateral damage and loss of life. The floodplain is defined as any land area that adjoins a watercourse or body of water that is subject to inundation. These areas of inundation are delineated on flood insurance maps and flood boundary and floodway maps, which are published by the U.S. Federal Emergency Management Agency as part of the National Flood Insurance Program. The U.S. Geological Survey also publishes flood-prone area quadrangle maps and the U.S. Army Corps of Engineers publishes floodplain information reports. The importance of these maps is obvious.

## Do Your Homework!

Thorough research is essential to effective community planning. Going the extra mile during the research phase, or following up on that nagging question may make all the difference. The sources you should consult will depend on the scale of the task as well as the goal you are trying to achieve. This section is meant to give you some direction; a place to start. If you are new to the game, you will become more familiar with the kinds of questions to ask as

**Figure 2.8** Floodplain map.

you gain experience. Do not be afraid to do too much research at first. Better to do too much than not enough.

If you are a seasoned professional, do not get too complacent. An old dog can learn new tricks. The old saying, "Pride goes...before a fall"[7] can be applied to many professionals who overlooked some essential element in the haste to get the job done.

Because our communities are continually evolving, the romance with the past and the deficits ascribed to the present are but snapshots in time. The communities of the future will combine the best of what we have learned only if we avoid planning them in a vacuum. Understanding this, the importance of the research phase becomes self-evident. The sources we have briefly described, as well as those you will find on your own, provide not only context and continuity but insight with regard to the community as a whole and the growth patterns we have established for it.

[7]Proverbs: 16:18.

# CHAPTER 3

# What's the Process? From Concept to Implementation

In Chapter 2 we identified the types of information we should review in order to responsibly undertake the process of community planning. Now we need to discuss the process itself and the products that result from it.

Our process requires cooperation among designers, financial, economic and real estate professionals, municipal authorities, and the community at large. Because growth is such a politically charged issue for many burgeoning communities, for any planning effort to succeed a team approach is essential. The design team may vary but should include a landscape architect, a civil engineer, and an architect. Nondesign-team members will include an environmental scientist and land surveyor, an attorney, an economic analyst, a real estate broker, a banker, the landowner, and the developer. During the course of a project the team will expand to include the municipal planning director and his staff, members of the local planning commission, city council, and various review agencies of the municipal government. For planning that involves federal or state regulations, someone from a federal or state agency may become involved in a plan-review or inspection role. For example, wetland delineation must be confirmed by a representative of the Army Corps of Engineers.

For any community planning effort to be truly successful, it is essential that all those who influence the process be part of the team, especially the municipal authority, because of its crucial role as overseer of the community welfare. More and more, changes to our communities require some form of modification to existing zoning restrictions. Most often, these are granted by use of what is referred to as *conditional zoning,* whereby a city council will grant a variance to a particular zoning requirement in exchange for certain guarantees or *proffers* made by the land developer. For example, the developer may negotiate to pay the costs or a portion of the costs of extending public services (i.e., water, sewers) to the proposed development in exchange for the council's vote of approval.

The size of the team will depend on the scale of the project. Obviously, development of a shopping center on a small parcel would not require the same level of interaction as, say, a large master-planned community, but the planning procedure generally is the same. The methodology has three phases: the research and analysis phase, the design phase, and the implementation phase.

## Research and Analysis Phase

Typically, growth in the community happens on a parcel-by-parcel basis and is begun when a landowner, be it an individual or a corporation, puts a parcel of land up for sale. Before an interested land developer buys the property he or she may contract the services of a firm that specializes in land planning, to help define what opportunities exist with regard to existing zoning restrictions and how the parcel fits into the overall plan of the community. Once we identify which information we need, its usefulness depends on our analysis of it.

The first step is a market assessment of the needs, demands, and trends of the community as a whole. The sources of the raw data needed for such an assessment have been discussed in Chapter 2, but we recommend an analysis by a reputable economist of the factors pertinent to the specific project. For example, a market assessment to determine the need for additional housing would evaluate such factors as land area, zoning, number of houses available, and the number sold in the past five years; the price range, an analysis of economic factors, with special emphasis on the growth or decline of local as well as area employment generators, and the maximum number of persons presently employed versus the number of positions expected to be filled. From this, the economist will make certain assumptions by estimating the number of housing units needed communitywide and the market share that can reasonably be expected by the developer for the proposed project, based on its location and the type of product it offers.

Subsequent to this or possibly at the same time, the land planner begins the data-gathering step. Using the sources discussed in Chapter 2, a detailed knowledge of the site and its surroundings is generated in graphic form. The overall assessments made at this stage will be a crucial element in the objective decisions made later. While there is no hard and fast rule on how this data should be recorded and presented, we suggest the *surrounding develop-ment assessment,* the *existing conditions map,* the *site analysis,* and the *character analysis.*

## SURROUNDING DEVELOPMENT ASSESSMENT

This includes data gathered on present and proposed developments as well as physical and market conditions. This information should be organized so that it can be quickly and easily understood, because it will serve as a critical tool in determining the appropriate land uses and their locations. From it, complementary, compatible, and perhaps expandable land uses can be identified.

A full awareness of what is occurring, what has occurred, and what is to occur in the immediate vicinity of the site is invaluable information when in the process of deciding the highest and best use of a parcel. In addition, this map will situate the site in its larger geographic context so as to give a better understanding of its relationship to the other physical elements in the area as well as to those undeveloped parcels on which the subject parcel may have impact.

## EXISTING CONDITIONS MAP

This map identifies the site's physical constraints and attributes (see Sketch 3.1). It is an inventory of all site features and regulatory constraints. These include:

- Topography, geology, soils, and climatic information
- Plant and animal life
- Existing zoning on and off site
- Description of restrictive covenants, deed restrictions, or other governing design criteria such as local ordinances
- State and federal criteria for environmental impact on the floodplain, air, and water quality
- Existing structures such as buildings, streets, and utilities
- Surface and subsurface drainage (hydrology)
- Unique features such as wetlands, archaeological, or historic sites

This purely objective information is used as a beginning point for the next level of analysis.

## SITE ANALYSIS

This combines the hard objective data of the existing conditions map (geology, topography, hydrology, soils, vegetation, wildlife, climate, utilities, and so on), with realistic opportunities and somewhat subjective and intuitive design considerations. This is the stage where certain observations and judgments can be made about the site with regard to access, circulation, entry, views, visibility, and orientation to surroundings, as well as existing and possible focal points.

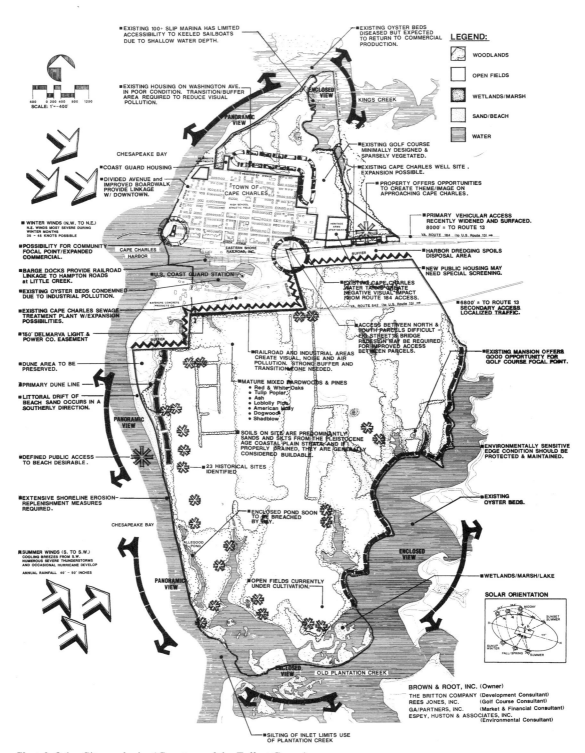

Sketch 3.1   Site analysis. (*Courtesy of the Talbot Group*)

# CHARACTER ANALYSIS

This assimilates all the data gathered into a purely subjective document that subdivides the site into apparent zones and identifies the inherent ambiance of each (see Sketch 3.2). This extremely valuable tool provides plausible justification for the location of specific uses in specific areas.

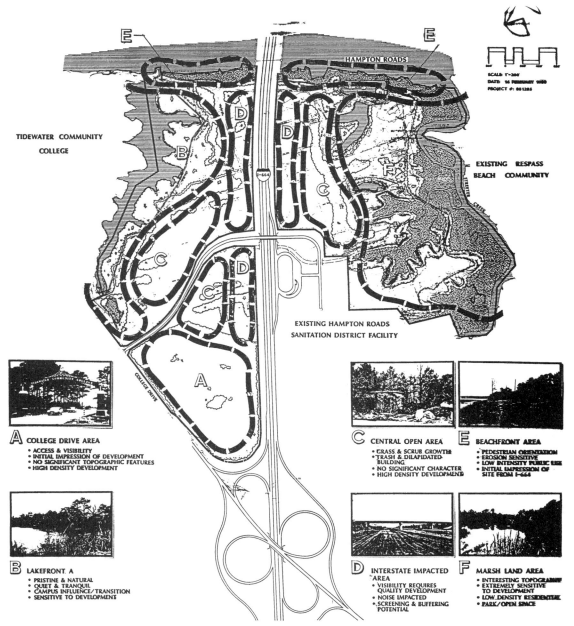

**Sketch 3.2**   Character analysis. (*Courtesy of the Talbot Group*)

The basic function of the analysis documents is to prove the viability of the proposed project to the financier who will provide the necessary funds; to the planning commission, board of supervisors, and city council to obtain approval and any zoning modifications; to the general public because, as we have discussed, growth can be so politically charged an issue that early involvement of citizen groups can help to reduce future conflicts. An informed public helps to reduce the possibility of misinformation and hostility to change that is often vented in the editorial pages of the newspaper, on radio call-in talk shows, and at city council and planning commission meetings open for public debate. The current controversy over urban sprawl and the advent of alternative concepts to control, stem, or refocus the tide of growth in our metropolitan areas has created an atmosphere where citizen involvement early in the life of a project is not only wise but prudent. The intensity of emotion, often fueled by the media, places the burden of proof of need for any project on the community planner. The analysis documents provide a source of verifiable data, not only as a design tool but to establish a criteria by which proposed development can be justified.

The final step in the research and analysis phase is the formation of a program definition. While clients may have a list of preconceived ideas they want to explore, it is the planner's task to clearly identify the goals and expectations for the project and blend them with the constraints and opportunities uncovered during the research and analysis phase. Ultimately, the program should relate the desired behavior or activities that are to occur within the subject site, place, or locale to the needs of the community at large. But it is more than just designating so many tennis courts and parking spaces; it encompasses both technical and aesthetic criteria.

For example, a purely technical program definition may specify that certain activities are desired (i.e., the creation of a park that includes 2 tennis courts, 4 basketball courts, 6 soccer fields, picnicking for 50 persons, a totlot, and parking for 75 cars). The aesthetic portion of this same program may outline the desired emotions that visitors to this park should experience (i.e., the park should provide a beautiful, relaxed atmosphere for family fun). While each portion clearly defines the park's goal, when they are blended together they communicate a true vision of the park's requirements.

Therefore, before beginning any design, an adequate program is mandatory. In fact, you might say, if you have a good program you have already begun the design phase. However, because the program forces one to focus on the project's intended goals, it should not be detail-driven or inflexible. It should be fluid and subject to change as new relationships are discovered and new opportunities present themselves.

## Design Phase

The design phase is the creative and problem-solving phase of community planning. It is the next logical step in the process, whereby we put the information we have learned about the market to the test. The task of *concept ideation* attempts to relate the goals of the program to the needs of the market and the constraints of the site. Simply put, it is the mechanism for creating order out of chaos. With time and experience, it happens at a fast and furious rate. The function of the human brain far exceeds that of the most sophisticated computers; therefore the designer, whether student or seasoned professional, has a uniquely powerful tool that can be employed to the task. Experience serves to hone the skills and increase the depth of knowledge by tempering intuition and wisdom.

During this stage innovative concepts are investigated by developing and refining alternative approaches or solutions that address the specific issues identified during the data-gathering and analysis phase. At this point it is good to remember that there is never one perfect plan—only better solutions! The optimum solution will probably be the one that best assuages the market-driven goals of the program and the concerns of the community, not necessarily the one that looks the best from a graphic standpoint. Also, the factors that influence the process change over time. Environmental regulations, the style of architecture, technological standards, the socioeconomic diversity of the population, and the needs of the market are all in a constant state of fluctuation. Solutions that worked in decades past, and in some instances even months past, may not adequately address the concerns of today's communities.

Alternative solutions in the form of freehand graphic sketch plans should be used to delineate land-use types in bubble diagram format. The positioning of these land uses ultimately will serve to enhance and facilitate a scenario of best possible compatibility with adjacent properties. The effects of each alternative should be identified and the concepts analyzed with regard to direct, indirect, and cumulative impacts on internal, adjacent, surrounding, and near-

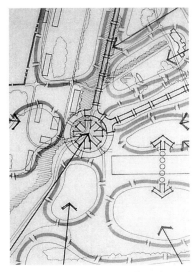

**Figure 3.1** Bubble diagram. (*Courtesy of the Talbot Group*)

by developments. The number of solutions you come up with will vary, but during the initial exploration it is not uncommon to create as many as ten possible solutions, many of which will end up in the trash can.

For example, one option may address the program's goals but fail to meet the needs identified in the market assessment. A subsequent solution may meet these requirements but fail to meet some technical aspect of the site-plan ordinance with regard to transportation; this might include the distance between traffic lights or the maximum allowable lot coverage as stipulated in the subdivision ordinance.

This, then, is the heart of the process and the key portion of the creative element: merging the research data, program goals, and site factors. You should refine your ideas into as many viable solutions as are needed, remembering that there is no such thing as a perfect plan—only a better one. After a preliminary client review, a final concept plan can be created that will meld the best elements of the three and can then be used for presentation to the client, to each of the team members, and during the various stages of public approval. It should be noted here that not all members of the team participate in the design phase. While all members have the opportunity to provide input at team review meetings, the primary planning roles fall to the landscape architect as land planner, the architect as artisan of structures, and the engineer as craftsman of infrastructure. Each member contributes a specific and necessary expertise to the team.

Once approval of the concept has been gained, the next step of the design phase is plan refinement or the *preliminary subdivision plan*. Using the broad-brushed recommendations proposed in the concept plan as a guide, the preliminary subdivision plan applies the specific criteria for development found in the site plan, and the subdivision and zoning ordinances, to create a more detailed representation of the project. While it can still be freehand in nature, it should be drawn to scale and with specific attention paid to the design criteria governing streets such as curve radii, parallels and tangents, and so forth.

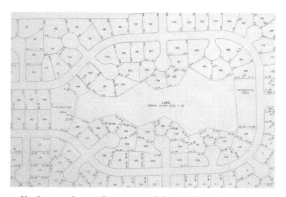

**Figure 3.2**    A preliminary plan. (*Courtesy of the Talbot Group*)

For example, elements of the preliminary subdivision plan would include numbers of required parking spaces, any landscape buffer requirements, maximum allowable lot coverage, stormwater retention or distribution facilities, location ingress/egress points, and so on. This stage tests the quality of the concept. A good concept will require very little modification. However, scaling mistakes at this stage may necessitate time-consuming and expensive changes later on, so be careful. Once complete, the preliminary plan is submitted to the municipal planning agency for review.

At this point, municipal planners examine the plan with specific regard to how it addresses and complies with established regulations in the various municipal ordinances. If the designer has done his or her homework, very few changes will have to be made. It is a good idea to address any questions that you may have during this phase directly to the individual reviewing the plan. This is also an excellent way to establish a rapport with your municipal planning colleagues. You never know when you might need a helping hand on a future project.

After the preliminary plan is approved, the hardline computation plan or *hardsheet* is produced. The hardsheet mathematically establishes or "locks in" all the elements of the concept in the two-dimensional plane. On it, all lines and curves are computed using known reference points such as established property lines or survey *benchmarks*. Benchmarks are monument points field-located by the survey crew that establish the horizontal and vertical elevation of a known point such as a large tree or manhole cover.

When creating a hardsheet for a parcel of land, the preliminary plan is used as a guide. By first calculating the centerline of the streets, and following the municipal regulations (i.e., minimum distances between reverse curves, minimum radii of street returns, cul-de-sac bulb sizes, minimum lot sizes, setbacks, etc.), it is possible to create an actual plan that will accurately represent the built product. It includes the *meets and bounds* of existing property lines, all public and private rights-of-way, and all major utility easements.

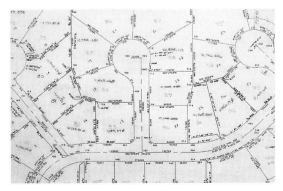

**Figure 3.3**   A hardsheet. (*Courtesy of the Talbot Group*)

This, then, is a second test of the concept's quality. However, even with the best concepts, it is not uncommon while creating the hardsheet to find subtle errors that were made during the conceptual phase. For example, in the process of finalizing a conceptual plan for a golf course community done by another firm, the authors found that the course had nineteen holes. A closer examination of the drawing revealed an additional number 9 hole and a number of substandard-sized housing lots unacceptable to the provisions established in the local subdivision ordinance. This type of mistake, although innocent, resulted in additional design costs to the client in order to correct a supposedly finished design before the final subdivision plan could be drawn.

The original plan was graphically superb, but, it lacked design substance. The thing to remember, therefore, is that a pretty picture doesn't always represent reality. But the opposite is also true; the quality of the graphic presentation can make or break a design concept. A timely and needed design solution may be rejected because it is presented with inadequate or poor graphic technique. Nondesigners have enough trouble as it is visualizing the final result from a two-dimensional drawing. Their task shouldn't be compounded by having to look at a poor graphic presentation. It is therefore paramount that review boards such as planning commissions and city councils be given the best possible product from which to base their decisions. Good graphics are very important but should not be used to camouflage a poor design. With the approval of the preliminary subdivision plan the design phase ends.

## Implementation Phase

With the design phase ended, the implementation phase begins. At this point, the hardsheet is used to create the *construction documents*. It would be appropriate at this point to distinguish the difference between the terms *plan, plat,* and *plot.* A plan is a method of action, a way of doing things, to achieve a goal. A plat is a recordable document that gives form and detail substance to the plan. A plot can refer to a two-dimensional graphic, either hand drawn or produced on a computer, but the word also is used to describe a piece of land, i.e., a plot of land.

Construction documents showing all the structures to be built are required not only to provide specific detailed engineering information on the project to the various contractors who may be involved but also to be placed on record and approved by municipal engineering review personnel so that they can verify compliance with city regulations. Section views are used to locate and establish the parameters of in-ground elements such as sanitary sewer lines, stormwater management facilities, water lines, and streets. During the preparation of the construction documents, slight modifications to the hardsheet may be necessary as a result of actual utility locations, turn-lane requirements, and so on.

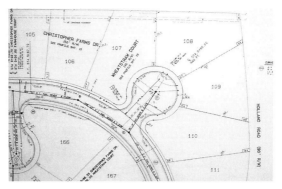

**Figure 3.4**  A construction plan. (*Courtesy of the Talbot Group*)

Site-specific construction plans represent a building or a configuration of attached buildings (i.e., a shopping center or an office building) on a single site. They will show building attachments, give topographic information for site grading, sanitary sewer and water hookups, street ties, landscaping and signage, and so forth. Subdivision construction plans are two dimensional, representing the plan (horizontal) and profile (vertical) alignment and elevation changes of site features such as streets and sidewalks, sanitary sewer and water lines, stormwater management elements such as manholes and catch basins, and so on. These documents graphically represent to the municipal review engineer that the proposed solutions for the site are not only efficient but have been designed to safeguard the public welfare.

The approved construction plans are then used in the bidding and negotiation phase in order to find a suitable contractor to implement the project. After a contract is awarded, the construction phase begins. A survey team is called in, initially to stake out, or establish, the elevation of the land form, then the location of sanitary and storm sewers, water lines, the streets and sidewalks, and ultimately the footprint of the building. As each stage is staked out, implementation can occur. The timetable for completion depends on the size and complexity of the project as well as a number of other variables such as product availability, weather, scheduling of subcontractors, and so on.

The hardsheet is used to create the *final subdivision plat,* which is an accurate scale representation of a proposed land use. It is used in formal presentations to public bodies and reviewing boards to gain final approval. The subdivision plat is the recording document that establishes property ownership, utility easements, and public rights-of-way. It is used to delineate individual parcels of property and is required by municipalities for recording land ownership and its transfer, and as the document of final design approval that goes into the public record. It is used as the basis for the field stakeout of the physical survey and to establish what is referred to as a *take down* or a portion of a subdivided parcel of land that is bought at a given time. For instance, a

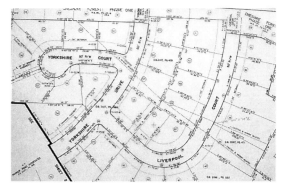

**Figure 3.5** A plat. (*Courtesy of the Talbot Group*)

client's attorney will discuss a loan with a banker for a certain portion of land recorded in a subdivision plat. The take down for this loan may be only 22.8 acres of a 100-acre site. The attorney can request a loan for only the amount needed to make improvements to that portion of the project. This method is particularly helpful to control the costs of phased development while maintaining legal land boundaries.

# CHAPTER 4

# Gotta Be Creative

Until now, we have discussed what community is and the general steps required for making changes to it. However, merely talking about the development phases doesn't necessarily tell us much about the creative nature of the planning process or how to tap into this aspect of the human mind. Until we understand how to harness our creative juices we will spend a lot of time spinning our wheels, so to speak, in an unproductive attempt to focus our imagination. But, once we understand this part of ourselves and how to put it into action, with a little work it can become second nature. So what is creativity?

Creativity, as it relates to community planning, is not so much a talent as it is the learned ability to solve a problem. It is learning to ask the right questions that enable one to see the big picture and identify a theme. Creativity is the spark that gives life to the raw elements. It is that point at which the "dead" elements of the research and inventory phase begin to come together and reveal design patterns. For the community planner, the act of being creative is a process of blending the program, that wish list of ideals, with the constraints of a set of existing conditions.

Creative thinking can be a struggle at first. The key to it, however, is to just begin. Whether pruning a tree, climbing a mountain, or creating a community, the first step is to take the first step. One must find the diseased branch or the one that is most out of balance with the tree and cut it. One must choose the easiest access to the mountain and go there! One must identify the "givens" of a site and utilize a theme as an underlying structure in the planning process. In each example, the first step is taken, then that step is assessed before proceeding. We might call this approach to creativity the STARR method: *ST*udy the problem; *A*ct on the finding; *R*eassess the situation; and *R*eact accordingly.

This act of being creative can thus be interpreted as *design*. For our purpose, the two words are interchangeable. Thus, creative planning is design and one who designs is a designer.

The act of designing is very inertial. The popular axiom, "Things at rest tend to stay at rest; things in motion tend to stay in motion" can be applied with ease to design. It is an active process. Inspiration may be difficult at times but that's why adherence to the program is so important. It can be the mechanism to help you jump start a cold brain. And, as any good designer can tell you, once the process of design begins it is like a freight train running downhill. It's fast and furious.

That's a simple enough description, right? But it doesn't tell us what design is.

The concept of design scares a lot of people, who infer some sort of mysterious art practiced only by the most gifted minds. Simply put, design is the conscious and subconscious mind wrestling with a puzzle, trying to resolve it. This process can be all consuming at times. In fact, you can get so absorbed in a particularly troubling scenario that you dream about it when you are asleep. Just because you leave the office at five does not mean you leave the puzzle at the office. In fact, the subconscious will keep pondering it so long that at some of the most unlikely times a flash of insight will occur and wham, you'd better have a pencil and paper handy. I have found that keeping a pencil and paper on the night stand is beneficial. That space of time between turning off the light and dropping off to sleep is prime brain time. Maybe it's because as I am trying to put everything aside for the night the usually mute voice of my subconscious can be heard. Or maybe I'm just freeing up brain space for it to work at capacity without so many interruptions. A word of caution here, though. Keep a flashlight handy, too. Let's be considerate of spouses who have to get up before we do.

Therefore, design is not a mystery at all. It is the graphic exploration of issues; a process of discovery that leads to the EUREKA!, that coalescing of ideas which is the act that sets mankind apart from the beasts...reasoning.

And let us not confuse the term *graphic* with *art* either. While some designers are artists, not every designer is an artist, and an artist is not necessarily a designer. We, as community planners and designers, draw to see the possibilities, to make the connections. Brain-hand-eye coordination allows us to see what we are thinking. The result should be a plethora of good and an equal number of bad solutions. But be warned: Design can be a messy business. We should have a pile of waded up paper on the floor to show for our efforts.

The goal, then, of this chapter is to encourage you to be a problem solver by equipping you with the tools that will help you define the issues and lead you down the path to discovery. We will also pass along some of our tricks of the trade that we have found to be the most helpful and that you will see utilized in the chapters to follow.

If you are an old hand at this process, maybe we can remind you of some of the basics. If you have been crunching numbers too long, maybe we can help you unlock some of your more intuitive skills that have been boxed up and stored in the attic of your brain. If you are new to the game, we can equip you with the tools that will help bring your best instincts to bear on the task. The thing to remember is that no one has the corner on intuition. While it appears to come easier to some, the rest of us have to work pretty hard at it. But in the end you will find that through experience you can cultivate a talent for it. The trick is to find what works for you and stay with it. To that end, the best way for us to help would be to show you what we do, and why. Hopefully, if we do our job right, you will be able to glean the best of what we have to offer and add it to your own bag of tricks.

## The Program

As we discussed in Chapter 3, the program is the culmination of what the client hopes to accomplish with his site as well as the opportunities that become evident from the research and analysis phase. It is the designer's responsibility to coerce the program from the client by asking probing questions regarding the vision of the end result. However, it is equally important to temper that vision with input from the ultimate users, if possible, as well as to meet the demand as identified by the market research. Moreover, needs must be separated from desires, as needs are *threshold* conditions while desires are *electives*. The program should be organized to segregate the technical requirements from the aesthetic desires. But it doesn't stop here. As the creative juices get flowing, the process of discovery may reveal new possibilities. That's why it is so important for the program to be flexible enough to incorporate new opportunities as they present themselves. As the designer focuses on the task of creativity, the program guides the action; it gives direction to that creativity, literally making something out of nothing. The designer's program works in the same way the program one receives at a Broadway play or some other special event works; it clues the audience into the sequence for the events they will witness and, in some cases, the goal that the performer hopes to achieve.

At this point we should not be overly concerned with the details. While it is important that your concepts be as realistic as possible in relation to cost constraints, your design should not be detail-driven. In fact, try not to focus on details at all initially. Deal only in broad generalities as you work through the design. You will find that the details tend to work themselves out as you further refine the emerging concept.

As in our example, the program must be formally written down so that you can refer to it often. In fact, to help you maintain your perspective, you should post it in a prominent place so that it can serve as a kind of checklist to keep you from forgetting anything.

So how do we get started? We have the program to establish our direction. We have analyzed our research data to identify the opportunities. What now? How do we jump start creativity?

## Inspiration

Design, much like writing, music, and art, is very kinetic; however, it sometimes needs to be helped along. Inspiration is the grease that can get the freight train of design moving, but it is not always easy to come by. It's true that if you have a good program the battle is half won, but calling up your inspiration is equally important.

There are three sources to which one can go for inspiration: nature, the manufactured world, and abstract thought. But as we consider these, don't expect us to create a new science. The goal is to get you to think in ways to which you may not be accustomed, to open your eyes to the obvious and the not so obvious. Every design we attempt should build on what we know already. This is not only smart, it is the way our communities have evolved and adapted over the years.

### Nature

The beauty of the natural world is unmatched for inspiring creativity in all but the most closed-minded. Whether it is the perfect geometry of a shell we find at the seashore, the playful sound of the meandering brook in the forest, the rich color of the desert landscape at sunset, or the intricacy of the veins in a leaf from a tree in our own backyard, inspiration abounds if we only look for it.

In the natural world we find not only beauty but economy of energy: doing the most with the least, with little or no waste. For example, it is no accident that a tubular column is the strongest structural element. Look at a reed or a tree trunk. In both cases maximum weight is supported by the least amount of mass. The cactus is another example. Its trunk and leaf are merged, reducing the surface area subject to moisture loss and thereby enabling it to survive in the most hostile environments.

The bubble is perfect in form and design. It maintains a perfectly round shape with an almost magical consistency. Each individual bubble, whether large or small, is exact in symmetry and proportion. Spherical as a single element, it takes on a crystalline, almost angular structure in mass. If you look closely enough, say at the froth of the ocean or the dishwater in your own sink, you'll see that bubbles take on an almost honeycomb appearance. This six-sided configuration, composed of six triangles (the basic building block), is the element which makes possible the geodesic dome of the Epcot Center at Florida's Disney World.

Nature abounds with energy and simplicity, providing multiple solutions to a common problem. The wings of a bumble bee and an eagle differ dramatically in size, structure, and composition; yet each performs its intended function flawlessly. Nature repeats successful solutions. It is no accident that there are no three or five-legged animals, but there are numerous no-legged creatures and multilegged ones.

Nature loves balance and symmetry. In every living thing nature attempts to create the perfect solution (body size and shape) to satisfy a particular problem (program). All trees of a species attempt to branch in a certain pattern (the perfect solution in a perfect world) but no two are exactly the same. Outside forces of wind, disease, and foraging animals all modify and customize in their own slight way each individual tree.

In the mineral world it can be said that beauty is a product of both strength and weakness. Erosion caused by wind and water exploits weak seams in rock, while hardened forms resist their inexorable, relentless efforts. The result: glorious valleys and sleepy serene deltas.

With nature as a guide, don't be afraid to think in ways that are new and unique. If a meandering stream inspires you to see a better hierarchy of circulation, go for it. If the cell pattern of a leaf leads you to construct a better town plan, hurrah! We need the innovation.

### The Manufactured World

It seems to be politically correct to find fault with all that is manufactured. Nevertheless, there is much to celebrate and imitate. As we look for inspiration in the manufactured world we seek to incorporate the best of human endeavor into the continuum of design. The successful communities of the past and present reflect not only the essence of our relationships with one another but the organizing elements by which we create form and function.

We have already mentioned Charleston and Savannah, which have capitalized on their historical significance, as well as such resort towns like Seaside, which has been given a lot of attention in the recent past as to what the communities of the future should emulate. But the point of this exercise is to ana-

**Figure 4.1**   Seaside, Florida.

**Figure 4.2** "Hamburger Alley."

lyze why some communities are successful and others are not. We need to ask ourselves such questions as: Why are some forms from the past still functional and desirable today? Why have the ceremonial boulevard and the traditional location of the marketplaces at key intersections of travel stood the test of time? Why do the resorts, the theme parks, the historic areas attract droves of us to their quaint and crowded streets? Is it not the economy of scale, the attention to detail, and spatial definition based on human perception that create a feeling of community? Do they not make us feel at home in comfortable relationship to one another and with ourselves?

In our travels as well as our daily lives we should constantly be aware of our surroundings, taking note of our reactions to the spaces through which we move. We can learn from the built environment by asking ourselves: What works? What doesn't? What could have been done to make it better? It is not enough to simply identify a problem; that's easy. We, as rational, thinking human beings, should always attempt to imagine a solution to the problem presented. Only through this active involvement with our manufactured structures can we possibly begin the process of eliminating those features that don't work; and if we can't eliminate them, then at least we can ensure that we do not employ them again.

As we do this we learn from both the successes and blunders of our predecessors, ourselves, and our colleagues. These are the true teachers, because their consequences speak so loudly. One need not look much further than the nearest "hamburger alley" to be faced with how *not* to do it. The philosopher spoke well when he said, "Those who forget the past are condemned to repeat its mistakes." I don't suppose he was thinking of community planners when he uttered those words.

*Abstract Thought...*
*The Emotional Connection*

Inspiration is not always limited to what we can touch, but can be inferred from emotion and feeling, which are abstract concepts. The psychology of

**Figure 4.3**   Smooth lines.

how users perceive a space or the community in which they live can have obvious ramifications. Research suggests that the quality of spatial definition affects perception and use. If joy and excitement are the desired emotions, as they might be in a community festival space, then the elements of bright color, quick changes of texture, and surprise should be utilized. If introspection and reverence are wanted, smooth curving lines and rolling topography should be used. The use of water, shade, and green color are calming, soothing, reassuring, while sharp angles, hard surfaces, and hot colors can render a place inhospitable for pedestrian use.

Concepts like perfection can be represented by certain basic shapes such as the circle and equilateral triangle. The grand buildings and public spaces that remain from antiquity in which we find these proportional elements inspire us with both their intricacy and their simplicity. Yet the key to their success and livability is their inherent ability to adapt to change. As each new generation embraces them, they continue to serve as testimonials to the emotions they inspire.

**Figure 4.4**   Rolling topography.

# The Language of Design

In order to think conceptually and communicate one's ideas graphically to clients, colleagues, and the public, one needs to develop a succinct graphic language. This language must both represent the various elements of design and visually describe the functional relationships of a place.

Nondesigners have difficulty interpreting two-dimensional plans. The "bird's eye view" can be confusing to the casual observer accustomed to experiencing the pedestrian scale only. Therefore, the plan needs to be descriptive and informative simultaneously. Every line should mean something and correspond to an item in the program. Simply put, the graphic symbols that represent the building blocks of community are the language of design. All the disparate elements of the built environment must be represented, using some discernible and distinct symbol. Each person can develop his or her own language but the key is to maintain a consistent repertoire.

If we are going to use Lynch's paths, edges, districts, nodes, and landmarks as building blocks of community, then we must associate them by a graphic designation. During the conceptual phase of the design process, each symbol should reflect its inherent activity and be bold, simply conceived, and convey the essence of the element in a very generalized manner. It must distill complicated patterns, land uses, and activities into very simple graphics that are easily drawn and readily understood.

We stress manual design over computer-aided design in the conceptual phase so that the designer can be in touch with the scale and shape of the site. It is very difficult to obtain the tactile interaction needed for the creative process while working with a mouse and a display screen, because they stifle spontaneity. The designer is removed from the design surface, and that can hinder his or her efforts. So, have plenty of pencils, markers, and paper.

*The Symbols*

PATHS
Paths are linear elements and represent both vehicular and pedestrian movement. They are free form, either continuous, dashed, or dotted with arrows to denote direction. Whether a major arterial or neighborhood cul-de-sac, an urban street or an undefined woodland trail, each should denote a degree of usage that is unique and clearly communicates proportion and hierarchy.

EDGES
Like paths, edges are linear. Because they represent boundaries that are either soft or hard, real or perceived, they are important organizing elements. They can be represented in a variety of ways including dashes, dots, hatches, or stipples.

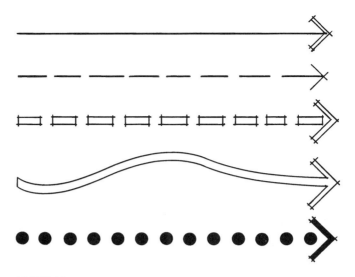

**PATHS**

Sketch 4.1

**EDGES**

Sketch 4.2

DISTRICTS

Districts encompass areas of commonality. Although less defined, they should be continuous, fluid, and graphically serve as a background for more focused, active elements. A pastel color wash works nicely for this, because it provides translucent substance.

NODES

Nodes are specific points of recognition. They are destinations and very often represent the core or center of a district as well as a transition between two districts. Because they are closely associated with paths, they can be represented by dashed circles or bulbs within a path.

LANDMARKS

These are important reference points. By nature they are *attention getters* and should reflect this special status graphically. Asterisks, stars, or some other symbol that screams, "Look at me!" are appropriate.

Other useful symbols include:

- *Buildings* can be represented by any number of geometric shapes, but don't get carried away. Keep it simple.
- *Trees* or natural buffers, can be represented by circles, fluid curves, or random continuous lines.

**DISTRICTS**

**Sketch 4.3**

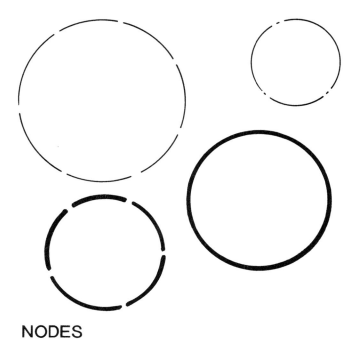

## NODES

**Sketch 4.4**

## LANDMARKS

**Sketch 4.5**

- *Screens,* whether natural or manufactured, can be represented as a jagged or picket-fence-type line.

- *Water,* whether a stream or the edge of a lake, can be represented by the universally recognized standard for water courses, which is a long dash and three dots; often the water surface is denoted by closely spaced horizontal lines.

- *Topography* should be drawn in two ways: existing and proposed. *Existing* topography is represented by short dashed lines, with every fifth contour shown slightly longer and heavier. *Proposed* topography is represented as a continuous line linking existing contours of the same elevation. Contours do not cross, as a rule, except when an outcrop is being illustrated.

- *Property lines* should be represented as series of long lines, with two dashes interrupting it at regular intervals.

- *Utility lines* can be drawn as a continuous line interrupted by the first letter of the utility being shown (i.e., "S" for sewer, "T" for telephone, etc.)

- *Views,* whether positive or negative, can be represented by two lines emanating from a point at the end of which is an arrow. An arc can be drawn between the lines.

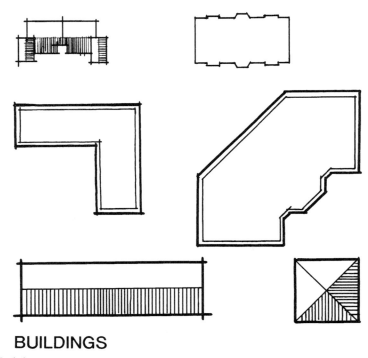

**BUILDINGS**

**Sketch 4.6**

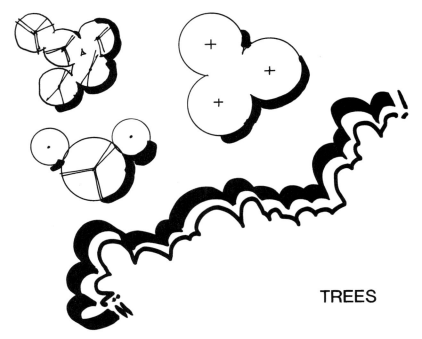

Sketch 4.7

## Design...How Do I Make It Work for Me?

Design can be very strenuous and energy consuming. It requires intense concentration to channel all of one's energy to the specific purpose of solving a problem. As we gather and analyze the pertinent research data, we are loading our conscious and subconscious mind with the keys to a successful solution. The techniques that follow will help you approach each new endeavor effectively.

- Get the pencil moving! You won't get anything done until you do. Right, wrong, or indifferent, nothing happens until this occurs. There is such a thing as studying something to death. Sometimes you just have to start slugging away at it.

- Starting slowly is best. There is no reason why one should not warm up to the effort. Just as a sprinter loosens up before a race, so you should spend a few minutes thinking about your plan of attack.

- Start with the elements of the site which are more readily and easily solved. In other words, work from the given to the unknown, from the general to the specific.

- Let your hand and eye react together, to the point where you are almost an observer to what is going on. Once you get going you can ask yourself if it feels good. If it does, ride the wave till it breaks (a little surfer lingo there).

- Look at the site in terms of circulation, open space, and structures, independently of one another. Optimize each system irrespective of the others. Then begin the process of overlaying each to identify opportunities and conflicts, ultimately blending them to an optimal solution.

- Make connections. Learning to see the connections between seemingly unrelated elements is a skill.

- Constantly questioning the status quo is the critical path to creativity. Always test yourself and your emerging solution. Ask questions like, "Have I missed an opportunity? What if I were to do this? Can I get another 10 percent here or there? What happens when I add, subtract, increase, reduce, intensify?"—Get the picture?

- Do not get too attached to any one solution, either. No plan is perfect. With each pass over the concept, a new piece of the puzzle fits into place. In fact, sometimes you find solutions to as yet unrecognized problems. You only recognize you have done it when you are evaluating your solutions with a critical eye. Serendipity is so sweet.

- Don't be afraid to leave a particularly challenging scenario when you are just not getting anywhere with it. It is better to take a break and come back fresh than to keep hammering at it and get frustrated. Take a break. Have an adult beverage. Relax. A lot of tough problems have been solved on the back of a cocktail napkin.

- If you are pressed for time and you can't afford to take a break, try walking around to the other side of the table. Rethink your approach. Readjust. Recalibrate your thinking.

- Think on your feet. Design should be done standing up. The phrase "thinking on your feet" is aptly spoken in the realm of design. Refining the details can be explored sitting down, but the initial thrust in the process of coming up with viable concepts and the key to good design is activity. And activity is best accomplished standing up.

- Learning to distill our creative energy within the movement of eye, hand, and arm is not unlike the athlete whose concentration is brought to crescendo in competition. A good designer should break a good sweat while designing. The exhaustion is invigorating.

- Ultimately we should ask ourselves how what we are proposing will fit into the community. What problems are we solving or creating? Is there a better way? Is the community supported, served, benefited, or enhanced? We have to consider the bigger picture, the larger issues. If it is good for the community, it is good for the individual, and the designer has done the job well.

- Always keep in mind that you are designing spaces for people to use; therefore, put yourself in their place. Let your imagination create the space as you visualize it. If you are aligning a road or street, try to get the feel of it as if you were driving on or walking beside it. If designing a park, place yourself in *that* park and look around. What do you see? What don't you see? What should you see?

- Don't be afraid to react to your own actions. At each step in the design process assumptions must be made. Pick a path and follow it conceptually as you steer it with the aid of the program. This method may lead you down many dead ends, but most assuredly you will not reach the appropriate solution without it.

- Don't overthink the solution. And don't get bogged down in attempting to work out the details before you complete the basic framework of the concept. Work from the general to the specific. For example, the circulation pattern of a neighborhood cannot be established until the points of access have been determined. Likewise, the house locations cannot be fixed until the lot lines have been situated.

- Have fun with the solution. If you performed your research properly, inventoried all the critical elements, and developed a design program, you're "loaded for bear." Your subconscious has everything it needs to do the job, so get to it.

CHAPTER 5

# Gotta Be Practical

Well now, after that pep talk about creativity we're ready to get to work, right? Wrong! We've got to be sure that we address the practical issues of the community to ensure that what we design can indeed be built. In fact, the absence of practicality has gotten many idealists into trouble. A client's ecstatic affirmation of a brilliantly delivered presentation can quickly be transformed into disappointment later on if our bombastic schemes of utopia are not tempered with common sense and a firm grasp on what it takes to get things done in the real world. Planning ought-to-be's make great discussion in the classroom and at the cocktail hour but have little impact on a limited project budget or a strained capital improvements program.

Conceptual thinking allows us to approach things from the viewpoint of a visionary, but that has some inherent danger. The same concepts that help us fully explore alternatives that may be beyond the purview of the program and the confines of the our budgets and technology, if not tempered with a firm grasp of the practical, can quickly bring our dreams slamming down to earth when we do the cost estimate.

On the other hand, while we know we have to come back down to earth, in the end it is worthwhile, for the sake of experience, to let our minds wander about in the possibilities of the way things could and should be. And let's not forget that many a problem has been solved by dreamers who dared to look beyond the obvious answers or the limited scope of a particular project. However, herein lies the danger. Too often we mistake our grandiose vision for innovation; our brainchild for the EUREKA! We forget that the true test of any conceptual plan is whether it can be built and, if it can, whether when it is built it will do what we claim it will.

## Public Utilities

In the real world, whether something can be built or not depends on how we address such concerns as the availability of public utilities like water and sanitary sewer service, the intricacy of storm water management, the environmental impact, and the adequacy of the current circulation system. The requirements for these services vary across the country because each region has a unique set of problems and opportunities. The extent of their availability is dependent on community needs and the density of development.

Residents of larger, more densely populated communities expect a high degree of convenience. Water and sewer service are expected and provided at a price, while the lack of adequate supplies of potable water can be a serious limitation to responsible community growth; so much so that many communities have had to place strict limitations on water use. The desert Southwest, for example, is no stranger to serious debate over water rights and the acceptable uses of water. Arguments over rights to the water of the Colorado River break out anew each time there is a drought in the states that depend on it for their water supply.

Sanitary sewer service can be a very costly part of growth, depending on the type of system required. Access to an existing system, its capacity, and whether or not it can accommodate an increase in flow, are serious considerations. Topography must also be considered. For instance, in hilly areas gravity helps to move things along, but in level areas pump stations are required to keep things flowing.

Smaller, more rural communities tend to be more self-sufficient. Well water and septic fields are the norm rather than the exception, and stormwater management consists of roadside ditches, farm ponds, and the local creeks and lakes. But with this seeming simplicity comes inevitable state and local regulations for lower density, to allow for adequate septic fields and water quality requirements for freshwater wells.

## Stormwater Management

All living creatures need water to survive. Humans, however, seem to place an extremely high value on its aesthetic quality. We pay large sums of money for houses on the beach, lake, or river. If we can't afford to own one ourselves, we rent one of these jewels during the summer so we can enjoy the restful, almost hypnotic effects of being "with" the water. There is no shame in it; it's historical. From the Moorish water gardens at Grenada to Lawrence Halprin's Ira's Fountain in Portland, from the fountains of Versailles and Vaux-le-Vicomte to the tumble, bubble, gurgle of the forest stream, we are entranced by water. But, when it comes to stormwater management we tend to approach it with an out-of-sight, out-of-mind mentality. We get so bogged down with the likes of the 100-year design storm that we forget it's still the stuff we gladly pay an arm and a leg to appreciate somewhere else. Until recently, the only concern about stormwater was how fast large quantities of it could be removed from streets and parking lots to prevent flooding. Now the quality of that water must be regulated.

When it rains, pollutants from lawn and garden fertilizers, petroleum products, litter from roads and parking lots, soil, debris, trash, pesticides, and any number of other chemicals are washed into the storm drains of our communities. These pollutants end up in the streams, lakes, rivers, aquifers, bays, and oceans, where they affect water quality and marine life. The issue of what to do with stormwater became more complicated with the enactment of the National Pollutant Discharge Elimination System (NPDES) in November 1990. This new federal regulation requires local governments to reduce the amount of pollutants in their stormwater runoff.

It isn't our intention here to discuss the technical aspects of this procedure; there are others more qualified than we to provide those lessons. Our focus here is to highlight ways to make stormwater management facilities an asset, not just a necessity.

There are two kinds of management facilities: dry and wet ponds. A dry pond captures a large quantity of stormwater and slowly releases it until it is

**Figure 5.1**   Ira's Fountain in Portland, Oregon. (*Photo taken by Mendy Lowe, courtesy Lawrence Halprin*)

**Figure 5.2**   The tumble, bubble, gurgle of a mountain stream.

completely dissipated. A wet pond, as the name implies, holds water at a consistent volume, allowing only the excess to escape through an overflow pipe or over a spillway. Between storms, dry ponds, unless they are well maintained, can be rather unsightly as they collect debris and litter. Wet ponds, while they cost a little more to construct, have more potential as aesthetic and recreational amenities as well as wildlife habitats.

Too often, though, these engineered storm water management areas have more function than form. Drainage ponds and channelized canals can become community eyesores that need to be fenced and screened to keep them out of sight. But this is a terrific waste of a good resource. Retention and detention ponds can be used effectively as amenities and, when designed with a little imagination, can help to create healthy, functional wetlands with both vegetative and animal diversity for all to enjoy. In fact, regulatory and permitting agencies look with much favor on projects that address both regional stormwater management and wetlands replacement and mitigation.

As a sales tool, strategically located lakes and ponds are superior assets in the fierce competition among single and multi-family housing developments. Aesthetically appealing as focal points, streams and lakes can help establish community character and enhance the perception of the built environment.

**Figure 5.3**    A very utilitarian channel.

**Figure 5.4**    A visually enhanced channel. (*Courtesy CMSS Architects*)

**Figure 5.5**    A healthy wetland.

**Figure 5.6**    Stormwater retention basin that doubles as a park...an opportunity gained. (*Courtesy CMSS Architects*)

## Circulation

Circulation systems, both vehicular and pedestrian, are the essential wayfinding elements of the community. More than an exercise in engineering technique, roads and pathways can either serve as necessary evils, or as conduits for the lifeblood of the community to provide access, service, and security for residents. Superior circulation design creates the mental pattern, or image, of a community. It is the one element that truly creates individuality and establishes character.

The issues we have discussed are all important, but we must admit that community planning continues to be influenced predominantly by the automobile. You don't have to be a genius to look at our communities and figure out that traffic engineering has done more to subdivide our communities into commuter hell than any other factor. One need only try to get from point "*A*" to point "*B*" in any town for it to become crystal clear.

In larger metropolitan areas one can trace the sequence of development back to a central core grid system. After World War II a modified or flexible grid came into fashion, due in part to its successful use at a planned unit

**Figure 5.7** Circulation as a necessary evil. (*Courtesy CMSS Architects*)

development (PUD) in New York called Levittown. This in itself was a radical break with the tradition of the times. In the sixties and seventies PUDs came to be more accepted, with far-reaching changes affecting society at the time. Curvilinear roads, looping collector streets, short, curving cul-de-sacs, and a reliance on the hierarchical system became commonplace. This approach worked well until the PUDs in a given area began to build out and the inevitable traffic congestion resulted.

In the 1980s, the exclusive community came into vogue. Every development had to be a *private* this or a *lifestyle* that, complete with gatehouses, both real and ceremonial. These usually relied on a single entry point that led to a large-loop collector road, with smaller imitations of the larger concept serving as the pattern for the individual neighborhoods. The 1990s find us looking back to a simpler time and place. The neotraditional town exhibits the traditional values of neighbors, friends, and family, with a deemphasis on the automobile and an attempt to enhance the pedestrian environment and promote mass transit.

Vehicular circulation consumes perhaps an average of 30 percent of our developed areas. It is the most expensive feature of community development,

**Figure 5.8** Roads respond to topography. Lynncove Viaduct at Grandfather Mountain near Blowing Rock, N.C. (*Courtesy National Park Service*)

**Figure 5.9**    An intimate residential street versus...

**Figure 5.10**    ...a residential microfreeway.

and it creates vast expanses of pavement that are literally a no-man's-land for pedestrians. But lest you confuse us with the frenzied whackos who believe that the automobile is inherently evil and is destroying the planet, let's approach it from a rational standpoint. Down deep we all know the real problem lies not with our cars but with the way our towns and cities are structured.

Because the automobile is such a strong influence and promises to be so for a long time to come, roads and parking must be approached calmly and logically. This is one of those situations when a little dreaming can be helpful. We've seen what traffic engineering has given us: the Los Angeles Freeway, the Atlanta Loop, I-95 through New York City, the Washington Beltway, etc., etc. Good circulation responds to topography, water bodies, wetlands, and public utilities to enhance movement within the community. Properly utilized, it can create harmonious unity to reinforce variety and wayfinding. But if used incorrectly, circulation does a very good job of creating discord and confusion. The problem is that too often it is patterned after highway standards, and results in very costly, inflexible design. In addition, the local circulation tends to follow or respect zoning lines just as much as it does parcel lines, which, in fact, reinforce the separation of uses and, consequently, community divisiveness. A better approach would be to balance street design requirements for safe and efficient movement with the scale of the application. For example, residential streets should be intimate, foster interaction among neighbors, and should be designed or customized for the community conditions. They should not be microfreeways.

### Basic Patterns

On a neighborhood scale, circulation patterns in our developed areas generally take on one of four basic forms: grid, radial, hierarchical, or looping. More typically, each neighborhood is designed using a combination of two or more of these basic types.

### GRID SYSTEM

The grid system attempts to disperse traffic uniformly as much as possible. It has been much maligned due to its seeming rigidity, monotony, and indifference to topography. But, hey, if it was good enough for the Greeks and Romans it's good enough for us! Seriously, though, we shouldn't be too quick to judge it on the basis of its misuse by traffic engineers and surveyors. (No offense, guys.) It can, in fact, be relatively easy to adapt it to topography. With its beginnings in the militia towns of the Greeks and Romans, it was easy and quick to construct; its primary aim was to allow rapid movement from one side of town to the other for defensive purposes. How ironic that given its beginnings, the grid system is now thought of in terms of congestion and inaccessibility, or gridlock, as it were. It was also used with frequency in the American Midwest where there was an abundance of level land. An extreme version of this street pattern is found in San Francisco, with its streets seeming to defy or challenge gravity by their *head-on* orientation, literally straight up and down the hills.

The success of the grid lies in its predictability of intersections, which gives the traveler clues and reference points in wayfinding. With the north-south streets as named boulevards and the east-west ones as numbered connectors, it becomes almost impossible to lose one's way. All one needs to be able to do is count. Moreover, in a grid system, because of the even distribution of traffic, practically every foot of frontage on the street is usable and functional, in that all the streets are directly accessible from the immediately adjacent, privately owned land—something not necessarily true in suburbia. A pleasant by-product of this even distribution of traffic is that there is less reliance on specifically designed collector streets, simply because they are not needed as much.

Exciting spaces can result when two grid systems converge. Again using San Francisco as an example, a walk up and down Market Street reveals interesting triangular intersections and green spaces. Overwhelming vertical spaces are created by the adjoining skyscrapers. New Orleans, with its grid

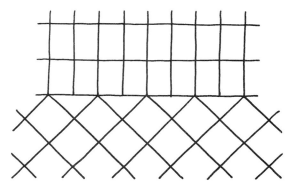

**Sketch 5.1**   Two converging grid patterns.

system bending in response to the shape of the Mississippi River, creates a physical and psychological link to that great waterway to which the city owes its existence.

The grid usually is very walkable for the pedestrian for reasons established above and the fact that it creates a variety of ways to go from one destination to another. However, repeating the block pattern too often can be very expensive and land-consuming. For example, when New York is mentioned, one thinks immediately of the world's largest collection of giant skyscrapers. But an equally astounding fact is that the island of Manhattan is perhaps 45 to 50 percent covered by asphalt pavement. All this, and yet there is still never a parking space to be had!

RADIAL SYSTEM

The radial system is a series of streets emanating from or focusing on a central point or zone. From a functional standpoint, this system usually originated in farm-to-market roads on which produce and livestock were transported to a central area for sale or shipment. This system works well to create a community heart or focus, thus functionally and figuratively unifying an area. It works best in combination with a set of circumferential roads creating concentric circles about the center. This, in fact, is nothing more than a modified grid system resembling a polar projection map of longitudinal and latitudinal lines. Radial streets allow the most direct route to and through a central point. In large areas these radial farm-to-market streets have evolved into the major collector streets, which carry the bulk of the traffic for the area and lead to peak periods of congestion at the central point.

While most cities have some form of radial system emanating from the older city core, this system has not been applied to the outlying areas and probably should have been used much more as a design approach. This could have helped create *focused* suburban areas rather than the sprawling format that has occurred. In some cases, this system has been superimposed over a grid to create some very dynamic urban spaces. Washington, D.C., Paris, and

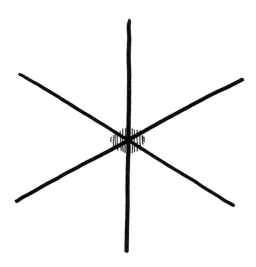

**RADIAL PATTERN**

**Sketch 5.2**

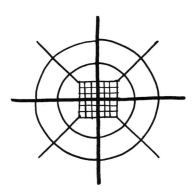

**Sketch 5.3**    The radial pattern with circumferential roads.

the original Daniel Burnham plan of 1909 for Chicago incorporated this concept as well as most of the more organic, less-planned core areas of cities such as Boston and London.

HIERARCHICAL SYSTEM

The hierarchical system, also known as the branching system, is a pattern of circulation structured much like a tree, in that smaller roads or branches lead to ever-increasingly larger collector roads. This concentration of traffic on fewer and fewer roads results in an eventual overload of the system, because it creates few, if any, alternative routes of access to a particular place. Instead, choke points are created, as there is essentially only one way in and one way out of an area. Because traffic is being directed to one or only a few points, circumferential movement around the choke points is very difficult.

**Sketch 5.4**   Typical hierarchical pattern.

This can also tend to isolate certain areas from the community at large, reducing their psychological link or incorporation into the fabric of the community. Hierarchical circulation systems came into design prominence with the advent of the large, planned unit developments starting in the 1960s, which persist in massive numbers today.

Hierarchical systems rely heavily on cul-de-sac streets, which can be used quite effectively when you want to "pull" some amenity, open space, or wooded area into a residential area. Neighborhoods that can boast of such amenities are usually those with higher-priced homes, as cul-de-sac lots tend to be more expensive. When used in large scale residential neighborhoods, wayfinding for visitors and residents alike can be exasperating, as all areas tend to look the same. This problem can be somewhat overcome if an identifiable spine road or collector loop is employed to create a discernible structure that literally holds the system together.

Hierarchical systems function best within small-scale residential environments consisting of a limited number of housing types and dwelling units.

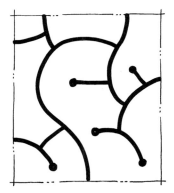

**Sketch 5.5**   Branching pattern can lack a sense of order.

**Sketch 5.6**   An identifiable spine road/loop road creates a discernible structure.

They also work well for areas adjacent to tidal waters, on lakes, or in areas of substantial topography. All of these areas are typified by an undulation edge beyond which no development is possible, making cul-de-sacs leading to collector streets the normal solution. By keeping through traffic to a minimum, they help reduce noise and conflicts between pedestrians and automobiles at the extreme end of the system. They are also very economical, as they allow the maximum amount of development area to a minimum length of street.

LOOPING SYSTEM

Like the hierarchical system, looping systems can be more readily utilized for individual neighborhoods than for communitywide application. When used in combination with the hierarchical system, a strong sense of place can be achieved for the neighborhood but, again, not necessarily for the overall community. Neighborhoods built using this format usually are typified by a primary entrance road that leads to a central, organizing roadway off which the residential streets stem. Because of their strength in organizing a seclusive neighborhood, they have been widely used in planned unit developments but can also be utilized very effectively within communities that embrace standard euclidean zoning. Despite the single-entry feature, this layout distributes local traffic somewhat better than the branching system, especially the further away from the entry one travels. For this reason roadway widths can be somewhat smaller than those found in the hierarchical systems. However, like the hierarchical system, all traffic is forced to a single point, with the same end result: traffic congestion.

To a limited extent this system can be applied in a linear fashion, especially in areas where large through-streets or highways bisect an area, with access to adjacent areas limited by topography, wetlands, or water. In these instances the primary role of such a system is to provide additional right-of-way frontage for development and to provide for a parallel access system to the main road. This form has been widely adapted to successfully create lin-

**Sketch 5.7**    Typical looping system.

ear office parks along major thoroughfares. It has been successful for this reason: exposure to and visibility from the main road is possible, while access to the office sites is channeled and controlled at fewer points, allowing larger traffic volumes on the primary roadway. However, what one gains from such flexible access one loses in the ability to identify a center or focus to the development itself.

As stated at the beginning of this section, neighborhoods and communities are structured using a combination or, more likely, all of the four basic circulation types. Whether for variety, response to topographic anomalies, wetlands, or in respect for the location of existing utilities, all can and should be utilized.

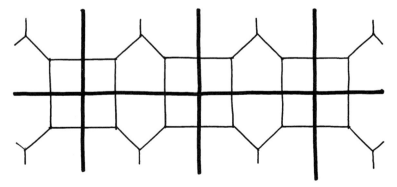

**Sketch 5.8**    "Mini beltway" around intersections separates through traffic from local traffic.

# Street Classifications

The function of a street dictates its classification. This in turn dictates its design volume and construction requirements. Streets can be either private or public; however, larger streets are more likely to be publicly owned and maintained. Residential street design standards vary among localities. On the other hand, more consistency is found with regard to the larger roadways due to the influence of federal highway standards throughout the land. One pitfall of standardization has been that many areas have lost their uniqueness, their individuality, and their sense of place. The alley has become all but extinct, now being found only in the older core areas. Alleys can sometimes be found, though, in fashionable redevelopment or gentrified areas, serving as a private rear access drive for upscale homes.

There are three types of streets generally recognizable within the community: minor streets, collector streets and arterial streets.

## MINOR STREETS

Minor streets are courts, cul-de-sacs, or short loop roads that directly serve residential homesites. These typically have a 40- to 50-foot right-of-way (r/w) width and contain two lanes of traffic, but are wide enough to allow on-street parking.

## COLLECTOR STREETS

Collector streets have a 60- to 100-foot r/w and are three- or four-lane roads that connect residential areas to community-center areas. At the lower r/w-width range, dwellings can easily be oriented to the right-of-way, but at widths above that they are oriented to side streets or sited with their backs to the collector. Commercial uses usually occur at the intersection of arterials and collectors.

## ARTERIAL STREETS

Arterial streets have r/w widths of 100 feet and larger. They are designed for the movement of high volumes of traffic between nodes with commercial or industrial functions. They are usually divided roadways of four or more lanes with a defined median in the center. Cross-access is limited to median breaks located at intersections and are 500 or more feet apart. Generally, no dwellings front directly on arterial streets. Dwellings that do face arterials usually are preexisting conditions; otherwise, they are most often accessed by a frontage road. This practice is expensive and not recommended.

# Design Principles

Street and roadway layouts have an impact on the community far beyond simply their cost of construction; they create the mental image one is left with after visiting a place. This being the case, they should be designed with special attention given to their appropriateness, orientation, and amenity potential. There are a number of design principles that must be followed to ensure that this occurs and that successful, functional, yet aesthetic, circulation is realized.

- Within the community there is a delicate balance as to the optimum amount of street with relation to lot size: The larger the lot size, the less total amount of street is necessary; the smaller the lot, the more street required. However, on a per-lot basis, just the reverse is true: Larger lots require more street and smaller lots require less.

- Double- and triple-fronting lots should be avoided. Double-fronting lots are those that front on a local residential street but have as their rear lot line the right-of-way of a major collector. Triple-fronting lots have the same characteristics as the double-fronting ones plus the additional frontage on an entrance road into the neighborhood.

- It generally is less costly, as well as less destructive to the land, to lay out roads parallel to topographic contours or at right angles to them. Otherwise, the diagonal layouts that are created are more difficult to implement and result in awkward building sites. In many cases their use cannot be eliminated, but in all cases they should be minimized.

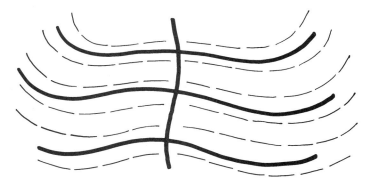

**Sketch 5.9**  Roads should be parallel to topographic contours or be perpendicular to them.

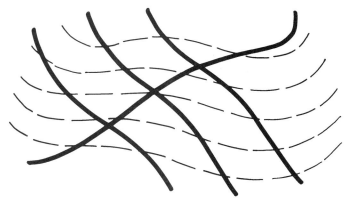

**Sketch 5.10**  Avoid diagonal layout.

- On rolling terrain, the terrain should guide the design to create interest and excitement. By simply following the lay of the land, a much more dramatic landscape can be achieved. On level land the designer must, through the manipulation of the road layout and structure location, instill a sense of drama or experience that comes naturally in areas with rolling terrain.

- If cul-de-sacs are short they should be of smaller r/w width—reducing construction costs and impermeable surfaces. However, overuse of cul-de-sacs at the expense of other minor streets should be avoided, since this practice can exacerbate traffic problems and require wider collector roads, thus eliminating any cost savings.

- Because circulation is the prime method of wayfinding, there should be an underlying order or logic to its design. Otherwise, chaos results. Too often confusion is purposefully created to inhibit cross-access and to force traffic to specific collector streets. Historically, emphasis has been placed on patterns designed to reinforce the separation of uses; however, this leads to further traffic concentrations that rely on just those few through streets.

- Conscious effort needs to be made to reinforce, not sever, the ties between residential areas and their supporting commercial and office areas.

## Design Considerations

Assuming that the primary network of roads exists in most of our communities, a wholesale redesign is neither feasible nor practical. However, new road projects and the development of raw land is continual, resulting in ever-increasing suburban sprawl. Therefore, let us discuss some of the finer aspects of road design. These points are not hard-and-fast rules that are required from a technical standpoint; they are desirable design approaches that can lead to a better community.

- Identify areas where roads cannot be placed (i.e., marshes, step slopes, historic or cultural places of significance, etc.).

- Identify those areas that are most suited to uses such as housing, commercial centers, offices, etc., and attempt to link them in as many ways as possible.

- Identify the most convenient access points and determine the desired lines of travel; that is, those points of desired destination from the site must be determined and internal circulation laid out accordingly.

- Promote access and land use integration within the community. In recent years road systems have been designed to identify individual developments from the outside and to discourage casual access from the local collector street. This might still be important, but we may need to reconsider or reduce this emphasis to promote a stronger connection to the community at large and to instill a greater sense of unity among various developments.

- Reemphasize boulevards. These wide, landscaped roadways create a feeling of grandeur and can easily be combined with an alley system. This dual system works well in high-density areas where the public street allows casual parking along the street, while the alley provides access and services to the housing, commercial, or office uses that front the boulevard. If land area and/or costs are critical, the alley can be one-way to reduce its size. When used in tandem with the alley, the boulevard width can be reduced, because the alley decreases the level of use required along it.

- Streets should be designed to keep the drivers' attention focused on the road and make movement easy and enjoyable. Simply because access between points "*A*" and "*B*" is required, there is no reason that the trip can't be pleasant and aesthetically appealing. Significant buildings, open space, entryways, etc., should all be considered focal points.

- Through traffic should be separated from local and residential traffic but should remain as a part of the community. Otherwise, dissociation from each occurs. A system that separates these two forms of traffic actually can reduce traffic on both.

- Superblocks—larger areas surrounded by streets but allowing no through traffic—were once hailed as the road system of the future. Originally designed to separate vehicular and pedestrian traffic almost totally, it is now thought that this is neither necessary nor advisable. Superblocks have proven to result in dangerous spaces for pedestrians and to increase traffic congestion in the areas that surround them.

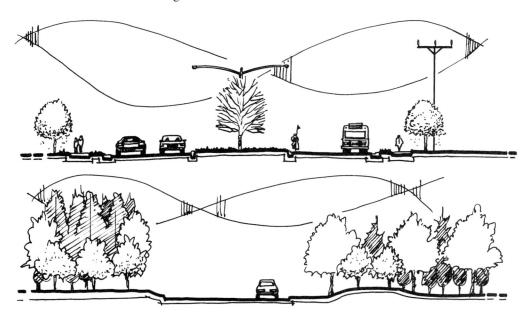

**PARKWAYS**
**Sketch 5.11**

- The concept of *friction* should be understood and applied with care. Friction is anything that restricts the flow of traffic by requiring vehicle stops and starts. Examples include: intersections, curb-cuts and median breaks, mail boxes, parked cars, and so on. Through streets and collectors require less, while residential streets tolerate more.

- Good circulation requires thoughtful consideration with regard to sight lines, transitions, wayfinding, visual clues, reference points, and so on. Circulation design should work to create an interesting and informative system that utilizes more subtle elements as well as the technical ones.

- The *visual grain* or *texture* of the surroundings should complement the design speed of the roadway. The lower the speed, the more texture can be discerned from the vehicle. At higher speeds, texture is more likely to be missed or unappreciated, making larger elements and spaces better perceived and appreciated at these higher speeds. This should be carefully planned and not allowed to happen at random. It is for this reason that the slick office tower adjacent to an expressway can be visually striking while at the pedestrian scale it seems strangely out of place.

## Technical Considerations

To this point in this chapter we have addressed only the grander design issues relating to the total community. However, there are a number of technical parameters that are either commonly accepted as standards or are dictated as mandates by the municipality. We attempt here to be as generic as possible; nevertheless, we must emphasize that every municipality adheres to slightly different standards that must be verified prior to any design.

- It is typical for most community streets to have right-of-way widths of between 40 and 90 feet, which usually includes a 4-foot sidewalk on one or both sides.

- Streets are usually crowned in the center for positive drainage, and may utilize a curb and gutter system or roadside swale to channel surface runoff to an outfall and act as a visual and physical barrier between vehicular and pedestrian spaces.

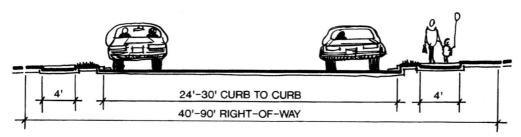

**Sketch 5.12**   Curb-to-curb and right-of-way distances.

- Curbing is usually 6 inches high, although a 4-inch rolled curb is sometimes used. Grassed swales and shoulders can be found in areas with low-density development.

- Pavement width varies; however, 24 to 30 feet from face to face of curb is common for a 50-foot right-of-way. A right-of-way of this width usually allows parking on one side of the street, while a 60-foot r/w allows parking on both sides of the street.

- Streets are laid out using a system of horizontal and vertical curves. Depending on the right-of-way width and design speed, the minimum centerline radius of a horizontal curve can vary from 75 feet for a 50-foot r/w to 250 feet for some state-maintained highways. Vertical curves provide positive drainage and enable the designer to adapt a road to the topography.

- *Broken back curves* and *reverse curves* usually are designed with at least a 100-foot tangent or straightaway between them to allow recovery time for the motorist and additional braking space.

- Intersections should intersect at right angles, but many cannot. It is considered unsafe, however, to design an intersection with less than 30 degrees of deflection. Also, intersections should be either directly opposite one another or at least 125 feet centerline-to-centerline apart.

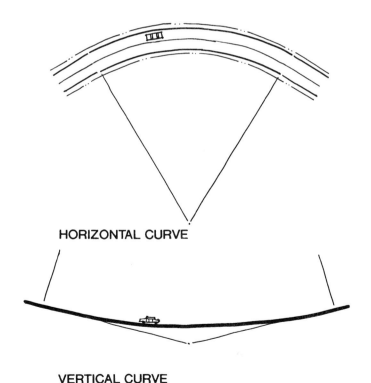

**HORIZONTAL CURVE**

**VERTICAL CURVE**

**Sketch 5.13** Horizontal and vertical curves.

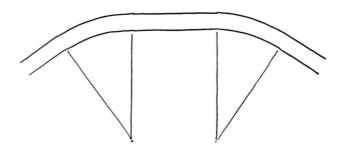

**BROKEN BACK CURVE**

**Sketch 5.14**

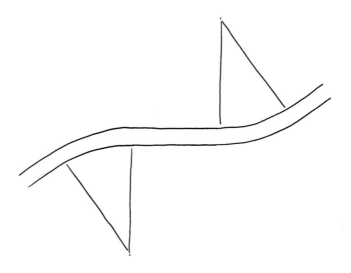

**REVERSE CURVE**

**Sketch 5.15**

- The curved section connecting two streets or *street returns* at intersections, should not be greater than 10 to 15 feet for most residential streets as measured on the right-of-way. A 10-foot radius equals a 20-foot curb radius. Why? This ensures that motorists are forced to stop when required and to make crossing distances for pedestrians as direct and short as possible.

- Cul-de-sac lengths vary but generally should not exceed 1000 feet in length. The right-of-way dedication of cul-de-sac bulbs or turnarounds usu-

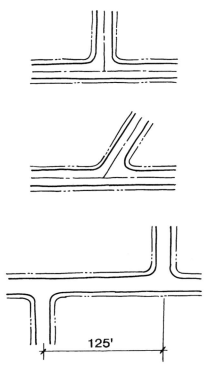

**Sketch 5.16**  Intersections.

ally is required to be 100 feet in diameter, with an 80-foot curb diameter. These are usually required for school buses, fire trucks, and garbage trucks, but should actually be considered on a case-by-case basis to allow flexibility and interest in the land plan. For example, on short cul-de-sacs, the school bus rarely accesses the street, remaining instead on the community collector street; therefore it does not require a turnaround sized to accommodate it. Likewise, fire trucks stop at the nearest fire hydrant; thus, on a short street they are more likely to stop at a hydrant location along the collector street. In other words, the standard solutions mandated by traffic engineers are not necessarily the best ones for a given situation.

- Other types of cul-de-sacs are *hammerhead, shunt,* or a modification of both that allows smaller vehicles to make a continuous circle but requires larger vehicles to back up. A center island with landscaping can dramatically improve the appearance of cul-de-sacs if the larger diameter is required. These, however, usually are frowned upon by municipalities because it is sometimes unclear whose responsibility it is to maintain them; that is, the city's or the neighborhood's. This should not necessarily prevent you from using them; just be aware that there may have to be some negotiation with city officials to determine whose responsibility it is to maintain them.

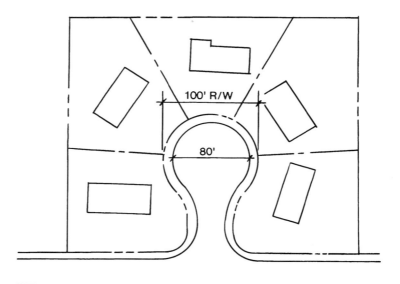

**Sketch 5.17**  Cul-de-sac curb-to-curb and right-of-way.

100' R/W

80'

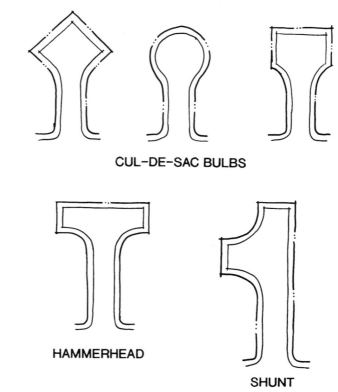

CUL-DE-SAC BULBS

HAMMERHEAD

SHUNT

**Sketch 5.18**  Cul-de-sac, hammerhead, and shunt bulbs.

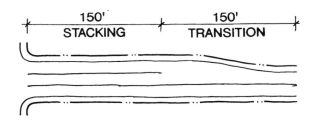

150'
STACKING

150'
TRANSITION

**TURN LANE**

**Sketch 5.19**

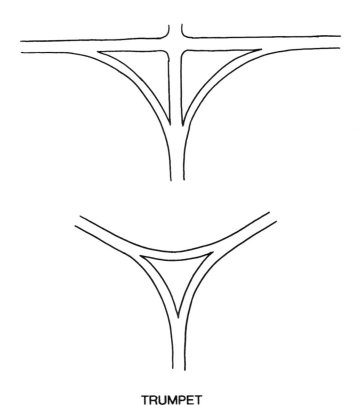

**TRUMPET**

**Sketch 5.20**

- The traffic generated by various uses (i.e., residential, commercial, office, industrial) must be considered when designing a road network for the community. Most intersections of minor residential streets don't require turn lanes, but larger intersections serving employment or shopping centers do, especially those accessed by divided roadways. A good rule of thumb for minimum requirements for these turning lanes is 150-foot vehicle stacking with 150 feet of transition space. This may require additional right-of-way dedication along a property frontage.

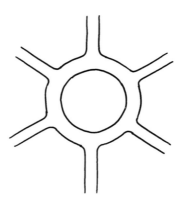

**ROTARY**

**Sketch 5.21**

- *Trumpet intersections* are an at-grade solution that allows some traffic to continue to move even when through traffic is stopped by traffic signals. These can also aid in creating a sense of place by providing space for entrance icons, and landscaping and water features.

- *Rotaries,* like trumpets, are good placemakers. Indeed, some of the more memorable examples of urban design contain at their heart a rotary intersection. Largely ignored and denigrated by traffic engineers, they allow single-way movement around a center island (focal point) and do not require signalization at lower traffic counts. Rotaries are especially useful for intersections of 500 to 1000 trips per hour and work well in residential areas, especially if the center area becomes a landscaped park.

- Intersections should not be placed on a high point such as a hilltop, and the gradient within 100 feet of intersections should not exceed 10 percent for residential streets and 2 percent for larger streets. However, if there is a choice between having it at the hilltop or slightly below it, the hilltop is the

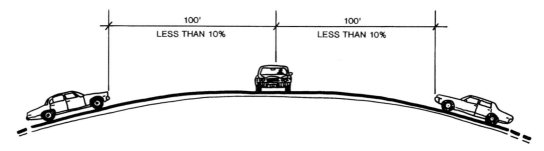

**Sketch 5.22**  Intersection gradients.

better place of the two because it has the better visibility. For similar safety reasons, intersections on tight curves should also be avoided.

These are just some of the detail design criteria in effect in most municipalities. The solutions offered here should not be construed as the final word on detail design. For that information consult your local engineering standards.

## Parking

Parking lots are perhaps the major contributor to the visual chaos that afflicts most of our urban and suburban areas. Accommodating the car has become the prime directive for most of our traffic engineers, municipal planners, and site-plan review personnel. Parking layout should be designed with *purpose* and *logic* that the motorist can instantly understand. Layout should be clear and somewhat predictable, with the focus limited to finding a parking space, not interpreting the ramifications of the layout.

However, too much of a good thing can have deleterious effects. To ensure an ample supply of parking, municipalities require an excessive amount of spaces, especially for commercial uses and usually for the peak use of only one week of the year, December 18–24. This mentality actually encourages more vehicles, more trips, and more pavement. Rather than solving the parking and traffic problem, this approach creates it.

For efficiency's sake, a parking lot is consolidated in as small an area as is feasible, with as many spaces grouped together as possible. In our commercial areas this has led to ever larger and larger parking lots, further distancing the shopping center from its servicing collector street. The result has been great expanses of asphalt or concrete usually filled to only one-quarter or one-third capacity for 98 percent of the time. The consequences of this fiscally irresponsible act include the fact that so much valuable land is literally wasted and put to unproductive use. In addition, from the environmental standpoint, the more impenetrable surface there is the more stormwater runoff occurs, which leads to either more pollution of local streams or, at the least, the consumption of precious land dedicated to stormwater retention or groundwater recharge devices.

The alternative is to build only those spaces truly needed to support commercial space or to build more retail stores in the space formerly dedicated to parking. This would not only return more tax dollars to the municipal treasury, but the commercial areas would benefit by enhanced visibility due to a location closer to the local collector street. Less land would be consumed for commercial uses, which would free up land for some other use, thereby increasing land-use efficiency.

The negative impact of parking lots can be reduced more effectively through dispersion rather than through the landscaping "bandaids" employed

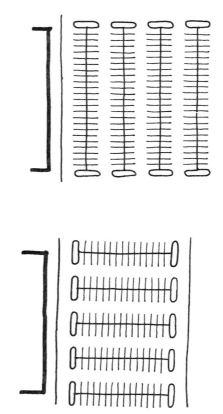

**Sketch 5.23**  Parking bays should be oriented toward the building.

by most municipalities. Although somewhat more expensive to construct, more parking areas with fewer spaces in each are aesthetically more pleasing. As a general rule, most people will not walk more than 300 feet to a destination. If applied, this knowledge would not only improve parking lot layout and create more efficient parking lots, it would also enhance the visual environment by eliminating the sea of parking we all loath.

In commercial and office areas alike, parking bays should be oriented *toward* the building; that is, the travel lanes should be perpendicular to the building's facade. This enables people to access the building entrance without crossing multiple travel lanes and parking bays. Psychologically, this ability to see the front door makes the distance traveled on foot seem shorter. The converse of this not only makes the trip seem longer, it requires people to walk between parked cars, creating a sense of apprehension and insecurity.

When multiple bays are employed or required, it is wise to include a landscaped island every three or four whole bays, if possible, to discourage motorists from moving across the parking lot diagonally. Such movements are a safety concern for motorists and pedestrians alike; cars approaching in such a manner are not expected and can lead to an overreaction on everyone's part.

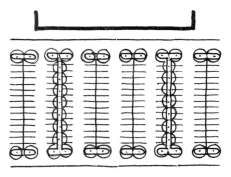

**Sketch 5.24**   Use a landscaped island every three or four parking bays.

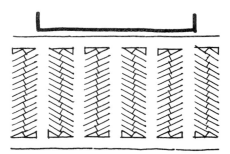

**Sketch 5.25**   Angular one-way systems are inefficient parking lots.

Such an island should be wide enough to support larger plant material, not only as much-needed greenspace in a typically inhospitable environment, but also for visual reference; it should extend the entire length of the parking bay.

*One-way systems* should be avoided to maximize space utilization and to reduce the confusion factor that normally accompanies such arrangements. Angular, one-way systems invariably lead to inefficient layouts and result in awkward triangular areas that are used for landscaping. Not that landscaping is bad, but this layout results in areas that are usable only for landscaping and nothing else. From a design standpoint, in these cases the designer is servant to the plan, not master of it. Besides, no matter how well planned the parking lot is, invariably a conflict will occur when a wrong turn is made.

Parking areas should have a *flow through* design where possible, enabling the motorist to exit from a confined area without reversing direction. Continual forward motion through a parking area is decidedly more preferable to a dead-end type, which necessitates backing up if all spaces are occupied. When long dead-end parking areas cannot be avoided, some form of turnaround should be provided. A small *hammerhead* arrangement can provide a convenient method of escape from a full parking lot, at the same time solving the problem of where to put dumpsters. In this way, the dumpster doesn't become the focal point of the parking lot. This solution works well for apartment sites. The true advantage of the arrangement, though, is that a turnaround can be provided with no loss of parking spaces.

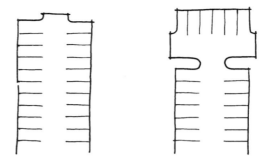

**Sketch 5.26**   A hammerhead arrangement is a good solution to the dead-end parking lot scenario.

If parking lot visibility is considered a negative, and the view of the building it serves is deemed a positive, it stands to reason that replacing the one with the other would improve the visual quality of our commercial corridors. Simply requiring that parking occur at or behind the building setback line, with no parking permissible between the building and the street, achieves a great improvement in the visual quality of our developing areas. This concept would also be useful for our existing corridors that front an overabundance of parking and lack the sense of scale and place that is so prevalent in suburbia. This is a good point to keep in mind when in twenty or so years many of those old strip shopping centers have outlived their usefulness and are destined for demolition. What a great opportunity to reverse the relationship and construct buildings that can provide greater visibility while improving the streetscape.

## Pedestrian Circulation

Getting people out of their cars and on to their feet is an issue that has been discussed at length in just about all the planning journals and has been the topic of a few books. Walking is not only the best form of exercise, it's the best way to meet our neighbors; and meeting our neighbors makes for better community. But it entails more than providing a sidewalk along every street, and more than establishing bikeways and fitness and walking trails along abandoned railroad lines, beside greenways, and in our parks.

Most of what we call pedestrian ways are pretty sterile and inhospitable environments, especially those located along busy thoroughfares. Extremes of heat and cold, sun, shade, wind, and glare can adversely affect use. Because of this you don't see many people using sidewalks in suburbia anymore. There's just something unnerving about walking along a four-lane collector street subject to wide swings of microclimate, with automobiles speeding by only a few feet away. It makes one feel exposed.

One contributing factor is that building facades are too far away from the street. The suburban building setback requirements rob us of the enclosure and scale that make us feel comfortable. And to compound matters, there is nothing separating us from the automobiles except two or three feet of grass, if we're lucky. The typical suburban street design sequence goes something like this: four-lane divided boulevard, sidewalk, 10-foot landscape strip (if you're lucky), parking lot, building. The kind of design sequence that most pedestrians prefer goes like this: street, on-street parking, sidewalk, building, parking. The difference that is understood by the pedestrian, albeit subconsciously, is scale.

Another problem is the absence of a reason to use sidewalks in suburbia. They don't really go anywhere people want to go, and if they did, getting there wouldn't be a pleasant experience for the reasons stated above.

Bikeways and fitness and walking trails, on the other hand, have their own unique problems. While they usually are located away from automobiles and parking lots, their relative seclusion and lack of a destination contributes to a perceived lack of security, discouraging use. As William H. Whyte observed in his study of small urban places, people want to go where other people are.[8] They are drawn to popular shopping, recreation, and entertainment centers to interact with and observe others. One need look no farther than the local shopping mall to see this in action. Jane Jacobs offered some insight into this phenomenon in her book *The Life and Death of Great American Cities*.[9] She suggests that there is a correlation between the amount and variety of activity associated with a sidewalk and whether people use it. She introduced the concept of networking of activities which, she explained, is the integration of both the amount of diversity included along the walk and the variety of interest it offers potential users. An *intricate mutual support* or *functional mixture* must develop before there is an incentive for pedestrians to use it. And, she stressed, the more diverse the activity and opportunity, the more pedestrians are likely to use it.

So, then, how do we put it all together to come up with a specific strategy for creating pedestrian ways that will be used? Here are a few guidelines:

- Remember the preferred sequence: street, on-street parking, sidewalk, building. Obviously, this isn't possible in every situation, but remember that pedestrians like spaces with an intimate scale.

- The ultimate goal is to meet the user's need for enclosure while providing a safe, comfortable, and interesting place to interact with others.

- Pedestrian ways should be integral circulation routes to specific destinations in the community. They must go where people need and want to go.

- Plan for novelty. Create alternate routes to the same destination. Allow for individual variation. People get bored if there is only one way to go.

---

[8]William H. Whyte. *The Social Life of Small Urban Spaces*, Originally published by The Conservation Foundation and now distributed by Books on Demand, a division of University Microfilms International, Ann Arbor, Mich.

[9]Jane Jacobs. *The Life and Death of Great American Cities*, New York: Random House, 1961.

- The concept of networking can be used to create a cohesive balance of function and amenity along the way. A hierarchy of social gathering spaces adjacent to or bisecting the pedestrian artery will enhance its usefulness.

- A choice of activities, both active and passive, provides something for everyone.

- Every location is unique. Avail yourself of every opportunity to enhance the walking experience. If we want people to get out of their cars, it has to be convenient, worthwhile, and perceived as a gain rather than a sacrifice.

# The Real World

*The next four chapters will depend less on formal paragraphs and more on bulleted statements and graphics. This will put the information at your fingertips and make this text a true handbook for design. The goal of these chapters will be to illustrate the way development typically occurs in suburbia, its problems, and some alternatives. The sketches should be used as tools for understanding the difference between the two approaches rather than as examples of the best and worst ways to do things.*

*It is not our intention to editorialize particular projects, but to point out the strengths and weaknesses of a concept as it relates to community design. The guidelines we provide should help you develop a critical eye, not just to help you recognize the problems in your own communities but, more importantly, to help you recognize what you can do to change them. Anyone can identify the problems that are the result of the way things were done in the past, but the pursuit of excellence in problem solving is a more prized calling.*

# CHAPTER 6

# Where We Live

Housing is the most prevalent kind of structure in any community. After all, it's where we live. Since the mid-nineteenth century, the suburb has provided consumers the opportunity to express their individuality and freedom of choice by offering a variety of housing types and styles. The diversity that is possible in suburbia is an ideal example of market forces dictating architectural styles and the amenities that accompany them. Although many variations exist, there are four primary types of housing:

- Single-family detached—still the most desired form of family living
- Single-family semidetached—duplexes, triplexes, zero-lot-line units, cluster homes, etc.
- Townhouses—the suburban version of the inner-city rowhouse; usually 4 to 10 units attached
- Apartments—low-, mid-, or high-rise

The concept of condominium ownership has tended to blend the various types of housing and blur the distinctions between them. It is not uncommon now to see developments of single-family detached condominiums, or even single-family detached fee-simple units, served by private streets.

# Development Patterns

*Single Family*

Single-family detached is perceived by many as the ideal housing type in the modern industrial world. It consists of a freestanding structure with yard space on all four sides. However, this form of development is the most expensive and land-consuming form of housing, requiring a larger amount of road construction, utilities construction, and land clearing. In addition, the increased runoff from the excessive road construction increases the likelihood of surface-water pollution.

Suburban *neighborhoods* are usually developed as a separate parcel following existing property lines, with only one or two points of access, and situated on the site in a random fashion. Since suburbia generally grows from areas of higher concentration toward areas of lower concentration, the density generally increases, not decreases, as development reaches farther out. Over time, zoning requirements generally call for a range of housing sizes in order to provide a variety of housing styles and price ranges, thus enabling the maximum number of people to be able to afford detached units.

*DESIGN PARAMETERS*

- Single-family lots usually range in size from 3500 square feet (SF) up to estates measured in tens of acres. Typical lot size thresholds are 4500 SF; 6000–6500 SF; 7500–10,000 SF; 12,000–15,000 SF; 20,000 SF; 30,000 SF; and 40,000 SF.
- A front-yard setback of between 10 and 50 feet usually is required
- A side yard of at least 5 feet or more (see Sketch 6.1a).
- A rear yard of 10 or more feet

**Figure 6.1**    Suburban neighborhood. (*Courtesy of CMSS Architects*)

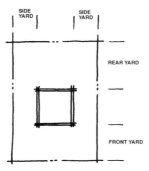

**Sketch 6.1a**   Single-family house and lot.

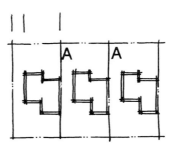

**Sketch 6.1b**   Zero-lot-line houses. The elimination of side yard (**A**) reduces lot size and cost to develop, with little or no reduction in house size.

## Single-Family Semidetached

Known by such names as cluster homes, z-lot or zero-lot line (see Sketch 6.1b), duplex or triplex, the semidetached single-family home is an attempt to provide affordable single-family housing to a larger segment of the population. This is accomplished by eliminating one of the side yards and building the house on the property line itself. In recent years many new and innovative forms have been developed in California, Florida, Texas, and a number of exclusive resort areas. Great effort has been expended to create living environments that are both spacious and functional, exciting yet practical. The goal of this type of housing is to incorporate as many features of single-family detached homes as possible, but at densities that approach those of townhouses.

### DESIGN PARAMETERS

- The lots for these units typically are 35 to 50 feet wide.

- They maintain both a front and rear yard although at least one side yard is eliminated.

- These are typically built and sold speculatively, so the buyer has a limited number of options or upgrades available that can be added to a basic structure.

- With densities approaching eight units per acre (U/A), the land plan must be well designed to minimize the impact of a potentially crowded site.

- Site amenities are mandatory if these units are to be marketed effectively.

*Problems and Solutions*

*TYPICAL*

- Forced minimum setbacks require front-yard parking. Requiring a home to be set back more than 20 feet from a street almost ensures that all off-street parking will be situated in front of the house. In larger lots this may not be a problem because of the distance between the house and the driveway; thus, the impact of the parked cars is minimal. However, in the case of smaller single-family lots, the streetscape is consumed by driveways and parked cars (see Sketches 6.2a and 6.2b).

- Two-car garages can consume from 30 to 75 percent of the building facade, seriously degrading the image of the neighborhood, especially in higher-density single-family developments. This results in overemphasis of the garage doors.

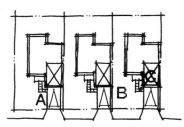

**Sketch 6.2a** (**A**) Minimum front-yard setback requires front-yard parking. (**B**) Typical architectural solution thrusts the garage door forward of building entrance, thus dominating the facade. (**C**) The garage door can consume 30 to 75 percent of the building facade.

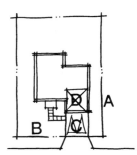

**Sketch 6.2b** (**A**) Zero-lot-line side yard usually contains no windows or doors to ensure privacy to adjacent unit. (**B**) Minimum front-yard setback literally requires front-yard parking. (**C**) Single-car driveway encumbers 20 to 35 percent of lot width. (**D**) Double-car garage encumbers 35 to 60 percent of lot width.

- Setback requirements and the need to accommodate automobiles has affected the architecture of single-family housing by thrusting the garage forward of the house proper, thus presenting the car accommodations in stronger light than the front door itself.

*ALTERNATIVE*

- Relax mandatory setback requirements to allow a house siting closer to the street than is normally deemed acceptable. This not only provides for a larger rear yard, but encourages garage door placement at or behind the house's facade, thus emphasizing the front door instead of the garage door. Ideally, placing the garage door 16 feet or more behind the facade of the house would result in the cars being parked between the houses rather than in front of them (see Sketches 6.3a, 6.3b, 6.4a, and 6.4b).

- Deemphasize the garage door by encouraging side-loading garages both on the larger lots and in smaller, higher-density situations. This can greatly improve this visually negative situation. This is encouraged only when it is not possible to locate the garages behind the front of the building. Direct vehicular access to the rear yard is also an added benefit of this arrangement.

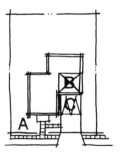

**Sketch 6.3a** (**A**) Reduced setback puts visual emphasis on building and not the garage door. (**B**) Recessed garage deemphasizes door and creates a parking niche, reducing emphasis on parked cars. (**C**) If garage is recessed enough, the automobiles can be parked behind the building line.

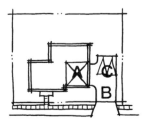

**Sketch 6.3b** (**A**) Side-load garage further reduces view of garage door. (**B**) Parking apron doubles as front-door courtyard. (**C**) Side-load garage allows forward entry into the street rather than having to back into the street, thus making the movement safer.

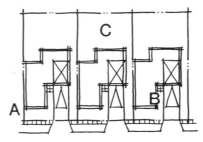

**Sketch 6.4a**  (**A**) Recessed parking reduces view of cars from the street. (**B**) Forwardly oriented front door increases street surveillance, enhancing safety. (**C**) Larger rear yard results from forward house shift.

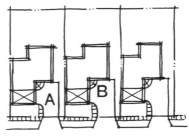

**Sketch 6.4b**  (**A**) Side-load garage allows continuous building facade, improving streetscape. (**B**) Side-load garage can allow vehicular access to rear yard in wider lots.

**Figure 6.2**  Homes should be closer to the street.

*TYPICAL*

- Smaller-lot scenarios result in unneeded tree removal to accommodate positive drainage, as mandated by many municipal engineers. In many communities, surface drainage must move forward from the rear of the lot to the front and must occur within the site boundaries. The method most often employed to accomplish this is the use of drainage swales around the house, typically following the side-lot lines and requiring the removal of any object in the swale's path, including trees. For adjacent lots, what

**Figure 6.3**   Emphasize the front door…Put the garage door in the rear.

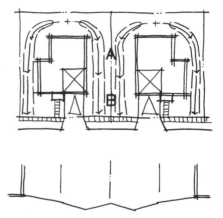

**Sketch 6.5a** (**A**) Typical design standards require drainage swales to be cut, eliminating all trees occurring in the drainage way. (**B**) Most of the area between the houses is regraded to allow drainage swales along both sides of the common property line.

results is twice as much land being disturbed to accommodate surface drainage along side-lot lines. Some filling of the rear portion of the lot to ensure the movement of this surface water is also normally required (see Sketch 6.5a).

*ALTERNATIVE*

- By encouraging combined or shared driveways for adjacent homesites and using side-load garages, less pavement is required for each house, leaving a larger infiltration area for surface drainage. This also orients the garage doors away from the street, deemphasizing the garage (see Sketches 6.5b, and 6.5c).

*TYPICAL*

- Rear orientation of homesites when located adjacent to a major collector street. These double-frontage lots usually require expensive landscaping

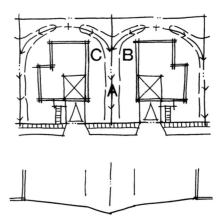

**Sketch 6.5b** (**A**) Combined drainage swales centered on the common property greatly increase the amount of undisturbed area around the houses. (**B**) More trees can be saved as a result of less land disturbance. (**C**) Amount of disturbed land between houses can be reduced by one-half.

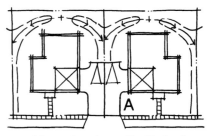

**Sketch 6.5c** (**A**) When used in conjunction with side-load garages with shared driveway, there is a greater potential to save more trees in front of the houses.

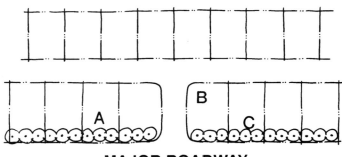

## MAJOR ROADWAY

**Sketch 6.6** (**A**) Rear of units overlook major roadway. (**B**) Double- and triple-frontage lots usually must have increased setbacks to distance houses from major roadway.

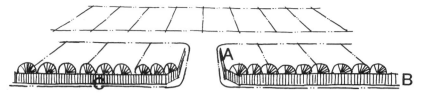

**Sketch 6.7** (**A**) Privacy fences 6 to 8 feet high present a negative image to the community. (**B**) Continuous fencing disassociates residential area from major roadway and makes the street a more dangerous environment. (**C**) More often than not, fences are not maintained equally, giving a deteriorating look to the neighborhood.

**Figure 6.4** Rear orientation of homes to the collector street.

and/or fencing just to make the homesites marketable, and even then they are most likely the last to be sold and built upon. And when finally developed, what is the presentation to the street? What is the legacy of the developer to the neighborhood? Usually a 6- to 8-foot solid wood fence built on the right-of-way line perhaps a mere 10 feet from the nearest travel lane of the collector street. This typical site-design solution has done much to disassociate neighborhood from neighborhood and reinforce the sprawl image of suburbia (see Sketches 6.6 and 6.7)

*ALTERNATIVE*

- Orient the sides of lots to the collector street and serve them with either a common, shared-access drive or a short cul-de-sac. This not only presents a better face to the collector street, it also reduces the number of lower-value lots that are impacted by the collector street. Flag lots are another method of accomplishing this within the bounds of most ordinances (see Sketches 6.8, 6.9, and 6.10).

- In the case of smaller single-family lots, the streetscape can be greatly enhanced by using alleys to serve rear-oriented garages. Coupled with a reduced front-yard setback and a reduced street width to allow on-street parking for visitors, a radical change in the image of our neighborhoods can be achieved. This is especially suitable for more urban areas or areas you want to become more urban.

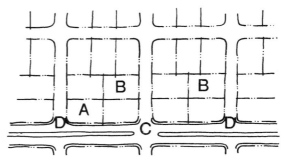

**Sketch 6.8** (**A**) Side orientation to collector street creates a better street and neighborhood image. (**B**) With a side orientation, fewer homesites are impacted by their proximity to the collector street, making fewer discounted lots necessary. (**C**) Median break defines primary neighborhood entrance. (**D**) Multiple access points to neighborhood diffuse traffic and reduce choke points on the collector street.

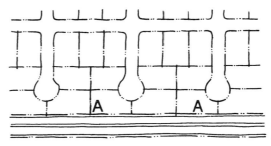

**Sketch 6.9** (**A**) If connection to collector street is not desired, the same side-yard orientation can be achieved by utilizing cul-de-sacs.

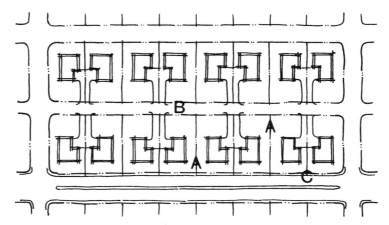

**Sketch 6.10** (**A**) Reduced front-yard setback makes homes more prominent on the collector street while increasing rear-yard size for greater privacy. (**B**) a 20- to 24-foot service alley provides access to rear garages or parking areas. (**C**) Lower front-yard fences improve the visual quality of the collector street.

**Figure 6.5** Fee-simple lots. (*Courtesy of the Talbot Group*).

## Townhouses

Townhouses evolved as high-density city housing. Originally serving as a transitional element between the commercial/industrial districts and the single-family areas, with the advent of suburbia the design style has been copied and applied in great numbers to outlying areas, where houses are clustered into separate, individual pods. Today their main advantage is that they function primarily as a means of enhancing density while providing more affordable housing.

Whether sold in fee-simple or as condominiums on a private street, this form of housing eliminates all side yards except for the end units. In most situations the townhouse is a two-story unit with a small yard and storage building. However, in resort areas where views are desirable, $2\frac{1}{2}$- to 3-story units are commonplace with attached single-car garages; in urban areas they are used to recoup high land costs.

### DESIGN PARAMETERS

- In years past it was common to build 10 to 12 units in a single block, but in recent years a maximum of 6 to 8 units has become the norm.
- The unit typically maintains a 20-foot front-yard setback from the right of way, principally to provide parking space for one to two automobiles.
- An equally sized rear setback is also provided so that the owner may have a small personal space.
- Common sizes range from a 14- to 16-foot minimum to a 24- to 30-foot maximum width.

### Problems and Solutions

### TYPICAL

- A typical 20- to 28-foot width for these units practically ensures that the entire front will be consumed by the parking pad and cars. In this case,

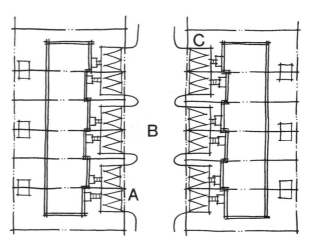

**Sketch 6.11** (**A**) Continuous off-street parking creates a veritable parking lot with few, if any, guest parking spaces. (**B**) The space between the building fronts is filled with 90 to 100 feet of continuous pavement. (**C**) Typical layout results in minimal front-yard landscaping space.

greenspaces and front yards are relegated to a 4- to 8-foot strip between the parking pad and the front of the building or a minor strip of yard extending to the street between end units (see Sketch 6.11).

- Automobile parking is always at a premium in townhouse developments because there are no guest parking spaces; essentially every space is designated for a unit. Continuous off-street parking leaves no on-street visitor parking.

- When more than six units in a row are used, the street image becomes one of continuous buildings separated only by an expansive parking lot. Pavement going from the front of one building to the front of another with very little green space creates the feeling of living in a parking lot. In many cases 90-foot paved areas between units face each other across a street. This number increases to 100 feet when a 60-foot right-of-way is required for townhouse developments, as it is in many municipalities.

- A rather severe streetscape results from providing two parking spaces per unit.

*ALTERNATIVE*

- The introduction of alleys for unit parking and service and the freeing of the street for visitor parking can greatly improve the visual image of the townhouse street. Coupled with a reduced front setback and a corresponding reduction of street width, the paved area between units can be narrowed from the typical 100 feet to 30 feet, and the front yard greenspace can be increased from 4 to 12 feet (see Sketch 6.12).

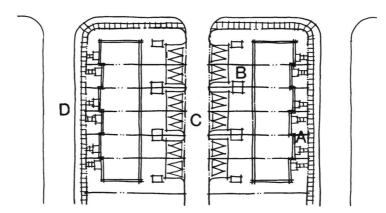

**Sketch 6.12** (**A**) Elimination of front-yard parking opens view of the building facades and increases landscaping space. (**B**) A reduced front yard gives a larger, more usable rear yard. (**C**) A sense of private access is enhanced when a rear alley is utilized. (**D**) A reduction of paved area between the buildings can be achieved even while providing on-street guest parking.

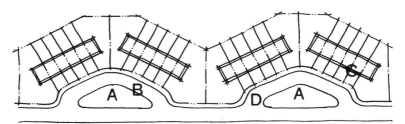

**Sketch 6.13** (**A**) A mounded and landscaped island screens parking areas and garages from the primary circulation. (**B**) Ample guest parking is available at the back of the landscaped area. (**C**) A varying building placement creates a visually more interesting and appealing streetscape. (**D**) A sense of belonging and shared interest is fostered by the common-access drive.

- When density is not the prime motivator of the development, variety in site layout can be achieved by incorporating an eyebrow form of parking and circulation. This method separates unit parking and access from the development's primary circulation. It also creates excellent landscape areas that can effectively screen the parking area from the internal circulation while providing ample on-street visitor parking (see Sketch 6.13).

*TYPICAL*

- Street orientation makes access to rear areas difficult from the outside for service persons like meter readers and repairers. Access must be across the adjacent parcels or directly through the unit. This can present a problem for such simple tasks as taking out the trash or cutting the grass (see Sketch 6.14).

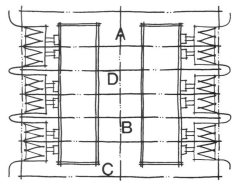

**Sketch 6.14**   (**A**) To accommodate the front-yard parking, rear-yard privacy is sacrificed. (**B**) Back-to-back arrangement allows second-story windows to overlook the corresponding rear yard. (**C**) Access to rear yards for interior units is possible only through the unit or across the rear yards of the adjoining units; a problematic endeavor when fences are involved. (**D**) When a 5-foot-access easement is employed, the result is usually an unmaintained, overgrown, and unprotected no-man's-land.

**Figure 6.6**   Access to rear yard for service is difficult.

**Figure 6.7**   Second-story window provides views into backyards of the units opposite, resulting in no privacy.

- Mandatory front-yard parking forces a building placement further back on the lot, creating an awkward back-wall to back-wall situation in which the rear walls of the two units may be only 20 feet apart, with the second story windows overlooking the yard space of the opposite unit.

*ALTERNATIVE*

- Where possible, primarily in condo situations, utilize side orientation to a public street with private access to serve garages, possibly rear loaded, relegating the front to either a public street or greenspace. A reduced-width public street provides visitor parking. While it appears that much additional pavement would occur in this situation, it must be remembered that private street construction is less expensive than that of a public street. This also solves the rear-yard access problem and can be accomplished with no loss in density as measured by the typical development scenario (see Sketch 6.15).

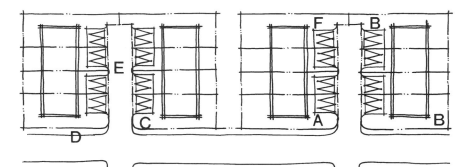

**Sketch 6.15** (**A**) Side orientation of parking to the public street reduces its negative visual impact. (**B**) Units can be designed with the front orienting to either the greenspace or the parking court. (**C**) The primary view from the public street is of the buildings themselves, low side-yard fencing, and greenspace. (**D**) Ample on-street parking is available to visitors. (**E**) Private street or public alley provides resident parking. (**F**) Garage parking is possible with a relaxed setback requirement.

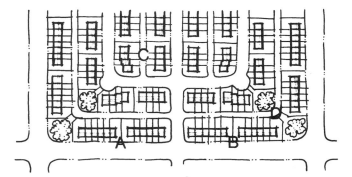

**Sketch 6.16** (**A**) Reduced setback helps to contain the street space by creating a defined vertical edge. (**B**) View from the collector street is of the building facade rather than the parking areas. (**C**) Alley provides resident and service access to units. (**D**) Corner spaces can be utilized as very accessible and highly visible neighborhood parks while improving the image of the intersection.

**Figure 6.8**  Rear-yard garages served by an alley system...

**Figure 6.9**  ...allow reduced front-yard setback.

■ If in addition to the more-normal-width residential streets the community collector street is not too large, 60 to 80 feet versus 90 feet plus, townhouses can be oriented directly to it, especially if on-street parallel parking is allowed. The units themselves can be served from the rear by either a private street or a reduced-width public street. The private street or alley, when utilized in conjunction with garages, can create a usable rear-yard space that is architecturally screened from the unit to the immediate rear. While this is not a new concept, its application in modern suburban America has been limited (see Sketch 6.16).

*TYPICAL*

■ Townhouse developments normally are designed as separate entities, freestanding and segregated from their surroundings, with little or no access between them and either higher- or lower-density residential. When ill sited, with little attention given to where they are located with respect to schools, commercial, or employment areas, they can seem extremely forced and totally out of place. In other words, their purpose as a transitional land-use element has been forgotten or abandoned (see Sketch 6.17).

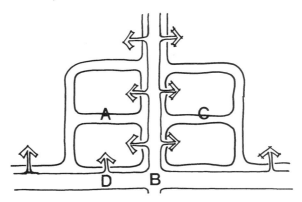

**Sketch 6.17** (**A**) Separation between uses is formalized, usually through an impenetrable fence or a nonvehicular open space. (**B**) Traffic is concentrated at entrance points to collector street, which creates a need for a traffic signal. (**C**) Little if any access between disparate uses is planned or encouraged. (**D**) Access to the commercial site from all residential areas must be from the collector roads.

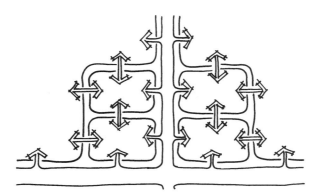

**Sketch 6.18** A certain number of cross-access points should always be provided between use areas to reduce traffic loads on the collector streets and encourage their use by through traffic. This access between uses can and probably should be formalized in a network of noncommercially oriented residential collectors.

*ALTERNATIVE*

- A certain number of street ties should be required to adjacent developments to better tie all housing areas together in order to establish and reinforce a sense of a community of various housing types, not separate communities of varied housing. It is not necessary to extend every street from one neighborhood to another, but enough to encourage a certain amount of interaction between neighborhoods. After all, prudent planning should require some manner of access between neighborhoods in the interest of fire protection and safety (see Sketch 6.18).

*TYPICAL*

- In too many instances the facade of a townhouse block is continuous and lacks architectural articulation. This is one element of urban design that is very often overlooked by developer and architect alike.

*ALTERNATIVE*

- Slight variations of setback, roofline changes and landscape enhancements such as hedges are elements that need to be utilized more.

## Apartments

With the exception of the core areas of the inner city where multistory apartment buildings are commonplace, most new apartments are two- to three-story walk-up structures. The garden-style apartments found in suburbia are designed to serve the needs of singles, young couples, and transients by providing starter living quarters at an affordable price.

*DESIGN PARAMETERS*

- Historically, access to the individual units was from a central corridor or breezeway. In recent years the trend has been toward separate direct access for each unit, or shared access with another unit to enhance privacy and create a sense of individuality.
- Structure height generally is related to concerns for fire safety and the height that can be easily accessed by fire fighting equipment.

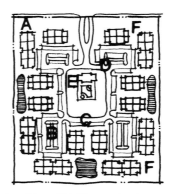

**Sketch 6.19a** Internalized parking. (**A**) Strong street exposure allows for highly visible landscaping and architectural design. (**B**) Parking areas are screened from exterior views. (**C**) Lower infrastructure cost with internalized services. (**D**) More direct access to entrance/exit possible with internalized parking. (**E**) Centralized recreation area is more accessible to all units. (**F**) Exterior orientation of structures maximizes off-site views.

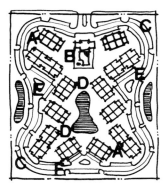

**Sketch 6.19b**    Externalized parking. (**A**) External parking requires increased set-backs for the buildings, which reduces the impact on adjacent properties and allows three-story construction. (**B**) All buildings maintain direct access to community building and recreation area without crossing any parking areas. (**C**) For residents, views of the parking areas are minimized, while for neighbors or passersby, the parking is fully exposed. (**D**) More flexible building arrangements are possible with external parking. (**E**) Higher infrastructure costs are probable with external parking. (**F**) For rear structures, access to the site entrance/exit is long and convoluted.

- Two basic principles apply to the site layout of apartment complexes: internalized parking or externalized parking; *ins* versus *outs,* if you will. In other words, the buildings can either ring the outside of the site with the parking areas internalized, or the buildings can be clustered to the center around an amenity with the parking oriented to the exterior. It is rare for one style to be used exclusively over the other. Most sites exhibit elements of both (see Sketches 6.19a and 6.19b).

### INTERNAL PARKING

- This method is utilized more often when proximity of parking spaces to the front door is an important feature.

- Because fewer parking spaces result when parking is oriented to the center of the site, this method usually is employed for two-story buildings with densities of 12 to 16 units per acre.

- Internalized parking is also employed when direct access to an off-site amenity is desired, such as a beachfront or a ski slope.

### EXTERNAL PARKING

- More parking is provided by orienting the parking to the exterior of the site making this method ideal for higher-density (16 to 36 U/A) three-story apartments.

- These apartment complexes tend to be on-site-amenity driven, with a pool, community building, tennis courts, and so on, with the amenities close to the building cluster.

**Figure 6.10** Site amenities are essential for apartment complexes. (*Courtesy of the Talbot Group*)

- Longer walks from the parking space to the front door usually result from this layout.

*Problems and Solutions*

*TYPICAL*

- The overwhelming negative impact of parked automobiles is the primary aesthetic failure in most apartment complexes. By focusing on automobile accommodation, an exciting, stimulating human environment is usually sacrificed. Immediately upon entering most apartment sites one finds oneself driving in a parking lot typically no wider than 62 feet from face-of-curb to face-of-curb, and driving in lanes 11 to 12 feet wide. If one lives at the rear of the site, and some of the sites can be very large, just getting out in the morning can be an arduous task.

**Figure 6.11** The overwhelming impact of parked cars.

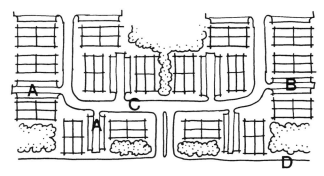

**Sketch 6.20** (**A**) Individual parking areas are designated for specific structures. (**B**) Individualized parking areas discourages use by nonresidents. (**C**) Internal community collector road provides direct access to entire site while enabling on-street parking for nonresidents. (**D**) Views along the collector road are of greenspace and building, not parking lots.

*ALTERNATIVE*

■ To reduce the impact of parked cars it is necessary to rethink traditional layout. This is most critical at the front of the site through which the vast majority of the vehicles must pass. Separation of the through traffic from that of the immediate units in order to reduce this conflict is the most effective method to accomplish this via stub parking, eyebrow parking, and sequestered parking.

*Stub parking* utilizes limited parking areas situated between individual buildings; these areas are accessed by an internal street or private road. This personalizes the parking for individual buildings and creates a stronger sense of ownership and responsibility on the part of the residents while discouraging unauthorized use by nonresidents (see Sketch 6.20).

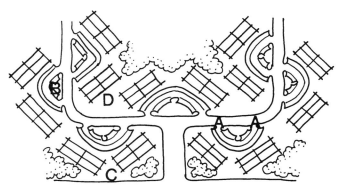

**Sketch 6.21** (**A**) Each parking area has two points of access to the collector road, facilitating traffic flow. (**B**) "Eyebrow" parking provides designated parking for specific buildings. (**C**) Landscaped island helps buffer parking areas from collector road, improving views. (**D**) Angled orientation of buildings at internal collector road creates more dynamic views of buildings and greenspaces.

*Eyebrow parking,* as in the townhouse example, performs in much the same manner as stub parking except that these parking areas retain two access points to a collector street and provide an opportunity for a significant greenspace between the parking and the street. The resulting configuration literally forms an eyebrow shape that not only separates the traffic but also creates a more dynamic visual orientation of the buildings, because few, if any, buildings front directly on the collector street. Instead they are arranged in an accordionlike fashion that forms large outdoor rooms that foster a sense of ownership by residents. The angular orientation of the unit to the roadway also makes this layout flexible and adaptable to irregularly shaped sites (see Sketch 6.21).

As the name implies, in *sequestered parking* different systems are established for both the immediate resident parking and the through traffic. Near the entrance of the site the two systems diverge, allowing through traffic unimpeded access to the rear areas via what in reality becomes a rather significant greenspace that has as a backdrop the apartment buildings themselves. An added benefit is that these apartments serve to screen the parking from the greenspace users and the through road (see Sketch 6.22).

*TYPICAL*

- Site layouts usually are very confusing, as the buildings seem to be randomly strewn about the site with little or no effort to utilize building placement to create wayfinding clues for the visitor. Few sites possess a site

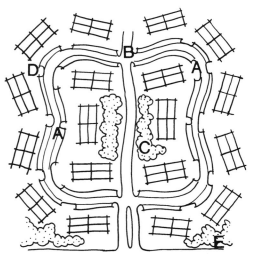

**Sketch 6.22** (**A**) Parking areas are sequestered or separated from the through traffic. (**B**) Through traffic to remote or adjacent parcels without interfering with local traffic is provided, with direct access to rear of site. (**C**) View of the parking areas from the collector street is screened by the intervening buildings and greenspace. (**D**) Building and parking placement is very flexible, depending on site boundaries. (**E**) Streetscape view from off-site is of greenspace, not parking.

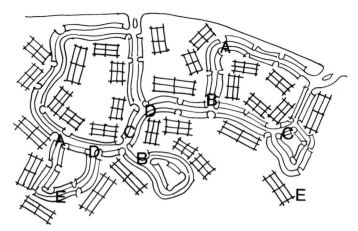

**Sketch 6.23** (**A**) Random street pattern confuses both new residents and visitors. (**B**) No sense of center or focus to neighborhood is created by site layout. (**C**) No internal collector-street system to facilitate traffic. (**D**) Continuous parking creates dangerous backing pattern and congestion near entrances. (**E**) Scattered building locations make security and fire protection difficult.

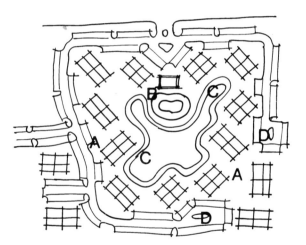

**Sketch 6.24** (**A**) Structured orientation of buildings helps to instill a sense of order and neighborhood. (**B**) Community center and pool serve as a visual focal point and neighborhood activity center because of their prominent entrance location. (**C**) Central stormwater retention and walking path serve as neighborhood binding elements as well as site amenities.

plan theme that can convey an understanding of the layout without actually experiencing it. In other words, most lack an order or structure that instills a sense of place and makes a site memorable (see Sketch 6.23).

*ALTERNATIVE*

■ The traffic and parking distribution methods can also help to create a sense of order and enable visitors and new residents to discern the underlying

**Figure 6.12**  Apartments should be sited to contribute to the overall street edge.

structure of the apartment complex that makes wayfinding easier while establishing a *site-plan theme,* as it were. In addition, this site plan theme imparts a stronger identity to the development, establishes a firmer sense of community, and enhances security and fire protection (see Sketch 6.24).

*TYPICAL*

- Because of poor layout, in many cases the parking spaces must be assigned to individual units to ensure that the tenants can park within a reasonable distance of their units.

- Poor building placement also results in ambiguous open-space areas that are not clearly perceived as being within the influence of a building or cluster of buildings. These "no-man's-lands" are a haven for criminals.

- On a more personal level, most sites are not organized in a fashion conducive to social contact between the residents, which can foster a sense of alienation and solitude, the antithesis of community.

*ALTERNATIVE*

- An additional benefit of the three organizing methods described previously is that parking spaces need not be assigned by number, for there is absolutely no question as to which spaces are associated with the units; the structure of the layout defines the relationship. Likewise, careful building placement "captures" the related grounds area, which enhances the sense of responsibility for the area on the part of the residents. Creating subareas, or clusters of buildings within the overall site plan, is a convenient method to reinforce this sense of responsibility. If a person has a feeling of ownership of an area, that person is more likely to be concerned with its use and take a more active role in monitoring it. The one thing a criminal dislikes most is a set of inquisitive eyes.

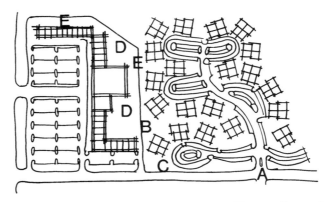

**Sketch 6.25** (**A**) Single point of entry concentrates traffic, usually requiring signalization. (**B**) With no direct access to either adjacent commercial or residential areas, the apartment site is physically isolated and psychologically separated from its surroundings. (**C**) Lack of defined street edge undermines the sense of enclosure on collector street, weakening the community fabric. (**D**) Commercial service area requires elaborate screening and buffering, further creating a sense of separateness from the adjacent neighborhood. (**E**) The spaces between isolated use areas become unmonitored and dangerous.

*TYPICAL*

- Apartment sites, much like townhouses, are very inwardly oriented, almost seeming to shun the surrounding community rather than becoming a part of it. Typically, they have only one point of access to a collector street, which serves to concentrate traffic in the immediate vicinity and more often than not leads to the need for a traffic signal. In addition to this, other off-site street improvements may need to be made, such as acceleration and deceleration lanes, median breaks with left-turn lanes, as well as additional travel lanes across the entire frontage of the site (see Sketch 6.25).

**Figure 6.13** Apartments often are sited just behind shopping centers, providing residents with a view of the service area.

- When included as part of a planned urban development (PUD), apartments are most often situated *up front,* near the arterial road system. Terms like *visibility, convenience,* and *easy access to interstates* may not necessarily mean that the building embraces the community. Structures may be more icon than inclusive.

- Another location often used for apartments is directly behind a shopping center but separated from it by the service lane—that void zone that accommodates such things as the occasional semitrailer, the dumpsters, and piles of wooden palettes or boxes. To screen this service bay, there is the obligatory privacy fence and customary landscaping. Fence and bushes notwithstanding, residents still have to contend with the view of the shopping center's rear wall, roof, ill-maintained fence, and the odor that a ripe dumpster can have on a hot day (see Sketch 6.25).

- In this situation apartments are used to act as a transition to such lower-density land uses as townhouses and single-family homes. While this is a longstanding approach, it shows that very little time was spent in the planning effort to integrate this transition housing into the fabric of the larger community.

- By locating apartments in *pods* with access to a street but no direct access to nearby commercial or office space, we are requiring vehicular access between two land uses that should encourage pedestrian interaction. Foot traffic actually is discouraged because the sidewalk is more ceremonial than inviting, and its proximity to speeding traffic and lack of enclosure makes it a hostile pedestrian environment.

*ALTERNATIVE*

- In the past, marketing strategies dictated that most new apartment developments utilize a single point of access around which elaborate landscaping, attractive signage, and a prominent clubhouse were located to "capture" prospective tenants. This has led to very isolated developments, which

**Figure 6.14**   Sidewalks in suburbia are often a poor pedestrian environment.

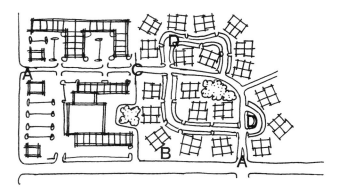

**Sketch 6.26** (**A**) Primary access from the community collector street serves as the marketing entrance, while the secondary access points facilitate the traffic and pedestrian flows to other land uses. (**B**) Building location reinforces the local street edge and the sense of enclosure for both the collector street and the apartment site. (**C**) Direct access to the commercial area from the apartment site enhances the commercial activity while reducing the traffic on the community collector street and the primary intersection. (**D**) Apartment site layout utilizes elements of both the eyebrow and sequestered parking arrangements.

project an almost aloof disregard for the greater community. While in many cases topography and other existing conditions require this orientation, where possible, closer networking with the surrounding street system should be employed to help to blur the transitions between land uses, especially other high-density residential such as townhouses or other styles of apartments. Most isolation problems occur when apartments are located in areas where the transitional residential elements are not present. A step in the right direction would be to first locate apartments in the most appropriate settings, where access to other housing areas is not detrimental. A clear sense of entry can still be established through the use of landscaping and signage elements at secondary entries, all the while providing alternative accesses and stronger ties with the community at large (see Sketch 6.26).

- Respect for scale and texture and the attention to detail are essential elements for street-front design. By maintaining an established street edge in terms of setbacks, and by transitioning the height of structures from off-site to on-site, the apartment complex not only will appear to function but will *truly* function as a contributing element of the community rather than just an isolated enclave snubbing it.

- If apartments must be located at the immediate rear of commercial sites, reducing the normal space between the buildings, especially those that orient to the street, can alleviate many of the conflicts. Minimum setback requirements to create a street edge for commercial buildings and the reorganization of parking lots is one step. Another is allowing more direct vehicular access, one that does not require the use of local collector streets; also, attention to more pleasant pedestrian spaces that do not require one to traverse an expansive commercial service area or parking lot. Transition spaces do not necessarily mean distinguishable edges that physically separate uses. The concept of community necessitates the networking of spaces to form functional relationships between uses and provides opportunities for maximum interaction among neighbors.

# CHAPTER 7

# Where We Spend

Before the late 1940s, following the convention of the day, practically all commercial services were located in *downtowns*. Situated at the center of town, at a major crossroads, near a train station or a river fork, usually on the most level land around, one would find a relatively dense, compact cluster of buildings with shops and offices on the first floor and apartments or offices on the upper floors. With the exception of the 5 & 10 cent store or the local department store, most goods and services were offered by individual merchants from their own storefront shops, a single service or line of merchandise per building.

The economic boom period which followed World War II was spawned by the reconstruction efforts directed toward war-torn Europe. It created unprecedented opportunities for growth and prosperity for the returning GIs. With the increased credit available and generous government housing programs, people began their escape from the crowded apartments located between the downtowns and the associated industrial belts that surrounded them. In greater numbers than ever before, they escaped to newly developed suburbs in newly acquired automobiles.

## Shopping Centers

What we now know as *shopping centers* sprang up along these routes into and out of town. Freestanding grocery stores and mail-order catalog stores were generally the first to identify the potential of inexpensive sites at the edge of town, large enough to accommodate both the building and the necessary parking to support it. This led to what has come to be known as *the miracle mile* of development, those commercial areas in what are now older sections of town with their chaotic variety of building shapes, sizes, and uses, identified by all manner of signs, each larger and more gaudier than the next. Usually only 100 to 150 feet deep, these sites consisted of simple, unornamented buildings with little or no storefront articulation, sited at the back of the lot with undelineated direct pull-off parking from the highway. All in all a fairly sterile environment, but one that addressed the issue of convenience (see Sketch 7.1).

Over time, however, these miracle miles eventually evolved into the three basic types of shopping centers we're familiar with today: *neighborhood centers, community centers,* and *regional centers.* Each center is practically ordained to its location by how far we are willing to travel for an increasingly larger selection of goods and the standing population in the immediate area. In other words, it is easy to predict which type of center will eventually be built, and generally where. People typically will travel one-and-a-half miles for food, three to five miles for apparel and household items, and eight to ten miles when price and selection are the primary considerations. While every locality possesses differing geographic and demographic anomalies that will affect its actual location, nevertheless, this spatial distribution can be expressed graphically in ideal terms by Sketch 7.2. In this graphic the small circles represent the neighborhood center drawing area; the medium-sized circles represent the community center drawing area; and the large circles, the regional center drawing area.

*Neighborhood Centers*

- Smaller centers designed to meet the day-to-day or immediate needs of a limited residential trade area of 2500 to 40,000 people
- Generally located at the intersection of a collector street and the entrance to a predominantly residential area
- Usually contain a grocery store anchor and sometimes accompanied by a drug store and several smaller retail stores and restaurants
- Average around 50,000 square feet, but can range in size from 30,000 to 100,000 square feet of gross leasable space, depending on the size of the local population and the demand for services
- Normally require 3 to 10 acres of land area

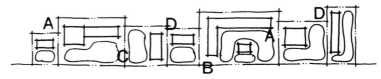

**Sketch 7.1** Typical layout of early commercial areas. (**A**) Varied building locations create a look of chaos and clutter. (**B**) Individual sites and signs compete for motorists' attention. (**C**) Access between parcels is rare, if at all. (**D**) Building orientation isolates areas at the rear of the commercial sites.

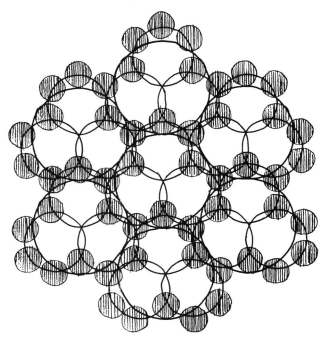

**Sketch 7.2**  Stylized spatial distribution of shopping centers.

## Community Centers

- Most contain all the services offered by the neighborhood center, plus a junior department store, discount store, and usually several more out-parcels than the smaller neighborhood centers.

- Serve a trade area of 40,000 to 150,000 people and are located at the signalized intersection of two collector streets normally four lanes each.

- Site areas range from 10 to 30 acres and provide from 100,000 to 300,000 square feet of gross leasable area. However, most provide at least 150,000 square feet.

- Other than the grocery stores or the junior department stores the normal building depths used to be in the 80- to 120-foot range. However, with today's merchandising philosophy of less storage space and more display space, lease space is generally in the 40- to 80-foot depth range, with a typical 20- to 30-foot storefront.

## Regional Centers

- A full complement of goods and services are available in regional centers, and include full-line department stores as major anchors.

- Typically contain 400,000 to over 1,000,000 square feet of gross leasable area on 30- to 50+-acre sites.

**Figure 7.1** A regional center. (*Courtesy of CMSS Architects*)

- With a trade area of over 150,000 people within a range of 10 to 15 miles, these sites have become the new downtowns of suburbia.
- The larger of these have enclosed malls and are located at the intersection of a regional expressway system and a community arterial collector street.

*Common Elements of Shopping Centers*

- Unified architectural design and treatment.
- Unified site either under single ownership or a development group.
- All shopping centers possess on-site parking for customers and are designed to be accessed primarily by automobile.
- Service areas are separated from the public parking areas and, therefore, the public's awareness.
- As a general rule in commercial development, building square footage consumes approximately 25 percent of the site area. Expressed differently, for every acre of land area roughly 10,000 square feet of commercial space can be reasonably expected.

**Figure 7.2** The service area is a no-man's-land.

- Each possesses a structured tenant grouping to provide a balanced merchandise mix. The various shops are consciously chosen to complement one another and minimize product overlap.

- To a greater or lesser degree all have pleasant surroundings, are generally safe in design, and contain some protection from the weather for the customer.

- All depend on automobile access for their success. It is true, however, that as our suburban areas grow, more people are frequenting their neighborhood centers on foot while preferring to use their car for most major shopping trips.

- The vast majority are almost completely separated from their constituent neighborhoods. That is, vehicular and pedestrian access to these centers is limited to the collector streets that serve both areas. These elements are not normally found in the conventional commercial district. A conventional commercial district, as mentioned at the beginning of this chapter exhibits more varied architecture, less manipulation of the tenant mix, and fewer on-site parking spaces. However, they almost always provide on-street parking, something strictly forbidden in the shopping centers we know today.

- Most provide a single land use opportunity—retail. Rarely will one find related or supportive uses such as high-density residential or office space on site. Instead, these are also separated from one another and connected only by their common four- to six-lane collector street or across expansive parking lots. By mandating a minimum number of parking spaces for each separate land use, this separation of uses leads to inefficient space utilization; thus it leads to more land area for the same uses that could be accommodated on smaller areas.

- Any new shopping center adds to the commercial stock of an area an amount of building area similar to that found in the commercial core of a small city. This is easier to understand if we think of each new center as the downtown of a town or city equal to the size of the trading area of the center.

- New shopping centers do not create new business; they can only pull business from existing centers—usually those in disrepair or poorly located as a result of changing demographics.

## Site Design: Points to Consider

*Location*

- The proper location is perhaps the element that is most closely associated with a center's success or failure. It must be easy, convenient, and quickly recognizable.

- However, the drawing power of a center is not due only to the distance to the next center but also to the convenience it offers its potential customers and the availability of desired merchandise.

- Conventional thinking has it that *neighborhood centers* must be located adjacent to a major collector street. This may be true, given the fact that major streets are the only practical means of accessing anything in our modern suburban areas. It is this mentality that created sprawl in the first place. But since they serve the local clientele, it stands to reason that these centers would not necessarily have to be so located; those who depend on these smaller centers for their immediate needs already know where they are located and what services are available.

- The need is greater for *community centers* to be sited adjacent to major roadways, because they depend on a larger service area and thus require more convenient access directly to the site.

- Drawing from an even larger area, *regional centers* need to be located close to a regional expressway system but not necessarily adjacent to it. If sited too close to off-ramps, merge lanes, and the like, access and maneuverability can be compromised, leading to traffic congestion and driver frustration. A distance of between *one half a mile* and *one mile* from the interchange seems to be an appropriate distance to a primary entrance.

- While it's easy to equate location with visibility, it would appear that too much emphasis has been put on visibility as a determinant of success and not enough on prior knowledge of a center's location. One never sees the Waldenbook's sign from the outside of the mall but one is sure of its presence. Most shopping trips are destination-oriented; that is, one usually goes to a particular store or stores for a particular reason. Few people have ever bought a refrigerator while out shopping for a pair of shoes merely because they saw an advertisement in the window.

*Configuration*

THE "STRIP"

- The strip, the simplest and possibly the most prevalent type, as the name implies, is literally a straight line of shops set to the rear of a parcel. Customer parking is between the building and the street, and service area between the building and the rear property line (see Sketch 7.3).

- Ideally, these should be no longer than 400 feet so as to keep all shops within an easy walking distance of one another. Some early centers, however, did not adhere to this standard and the result was some truly inhospitable spaces requiring extremely long walks. More often it led to simply moving the car from storefront to storefront, taking advantage of the overabundant parking.

- This is the form of most neighborhood centers and many community centers.

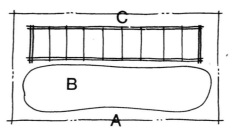

**Sketch 7.3** The *strip* shopping center. (**A**) Straight-line orientation of building is typical. (**B**) Parking is always located between the center and the collector street. (**C**) Service area requires screening and buffering from the residential area that usually occurs behind the center.

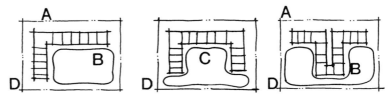

**Sketch 7.4** Variants of the strip center—*L*-, *U*-, and *T*-shaped centers. (**A**) Typical for corner location. (**B**) View from one leg to another shortens the perceived distance between them. (**C**) Midblock location is typical for the *U*-shaped center. (**D**) Full-block location with two-corner exposure usually results in a large strip or *T*-shaped center.

## VARIATIONS ON THE THEME

- Variations on the *strip* are *L*-, *U*-, and *T*-shaped building patterns designed to more efficiently utilize the parcel shape and to maximize leasable space (see Sketch 7.4).

- These occupy sites that are usually larger than simple linear strips and are more likely to be located at major intersections.

- Psychologically, these tend to make a large site appear smaller by encouraging the viewer's eye to follow the shape of the building from a point close to the access road at the rear of the site. A larger site so configured focuses attention on the building and not the parking lot, thus rendering the center more approachable.

- These configurations also make more of the storefronts visible to shoppers from the sidewalk, again making the site appear smaller and encouraging more shopping.

## THE CLUSTER

- The *cluster* is essentially a combination of the previous two types of centers arranged so that a purely pedestrian space results in the center. With the parking oriented to one side or completely encircling the buildings, the

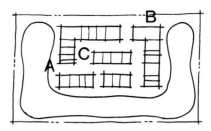

**Sketch 7.5** The cluster center. (**A**) Unless shops are double-fronted, the exposure wall can be unattractive and uninviting. (**B**) Perceived lack of visibility may reduce the marketability of the rear space. (**C**) Service to interior spaces is difficult.

interior spaces begin to resemble a small village or the traditional downtowns of small communities (see Sketch 7.5).

- This form has been adapted well to specialty centers that cater to a tourist trade that expects shopping to be an exciting event. Smaller shops offering a wide variety of small goods do well in these situations; however, the form does not adapt well to larger stores or anchors, which require larger service areas and visibility from the accessing road.

- This form is rarely utilized in today's suburban landscape.

## THE MALL

- The *mall* is simply the *cluster* configuration expanded and enclosed for weather protection. Initially, malls were designed in straight-line fashion, allowing an almost uninterrupted view the length of the space. Now they follow design concepts gleaned from an earlier time, utilizing small pedestrian spaces (30 to 50 feet) between the storefronts and using angles or turns to reduce the visual distance and focus attention and interest while traversing the space (see Sketch 7.6).

- Malls are the predominant form of regional and superregional commercial centers today. They have become the suburban downtowns, their huge parking lots completely isolating and separating them from the neighborhoods and communities that support them.

- Mall development has slowed in recent years because of overbuilding, reduced demand for commercial space, and environmental concerns.

### Parking and Circulation

- Most customer parking will occur within 300 feet of the storefront, and no parking should be planned that will be more than 600 feet away from the structure. People will not venture this far away except at the busiest of times.

- Parking should be orderly, logical, and easily understood, and its pattern should be discernible to the entering customer.

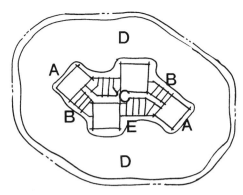

**Sketch 7.6** The mall. (**A**) Access to the interior mall through the anchor stores is encouraged. Direct access to the mall interior usually is limited. (**B**) Few smaller shops possess exterior exposure to the parking area. High, blank-wall architecture is the norm. (**C**) Small shops survive on traffic generated by the anchor stores. (**D**) A vast parking area separates the mall from all other elements of the community. (**E**) Exposed service areas are a natural by-product of the mall configuration.

- In most regional centers, parking is arranged in an angled, one-way system that both confuses and frustrates the parking customer. In addition, this style of parking is not as efficient as two-way right-angled parking, and therefore should be used only where site constraints demand it.

- Parking should be designed in the smallest increment or compartment possible; that is, through access-lane location, landscaping, walkways, surface drainage retention areas, or whatever; and the number of cars in a particular lot should be as small as is practical, given the cost constraints of construction.

- In the case of regional centers, it is desirable to plan parking configurations for no more than 800 cars. Likewise, these should be defined by access lanes, landscaping, etc. This can enhance the wayfinding ability of customers while making the entire lot visually more pleasing (see Sketch 7.7).

- All parking and travel lanes, landscaping, and walkways should be oriented to the building. No pedestrian should be required to walk through successive parking bays to access the store, and a person's path should be as clear of obstacles as possible.

- Circulation around regional centers typically is represented by a *ring road* located some distance from the building itself and travel lanes immediately adjacent the building. Given the fact that most parking occurs within 300 feet of the building, a better location for these ring roads would seem to be at that distance, to enhance access to those areas where parking will actually occur and to psychologically reduce the size and scale of the parking lot (see Sketch 7.8).

- Parking requirements for commercial areas are biased toward the high side in most site-plan ordinances. Rarely do they take into account the multiple

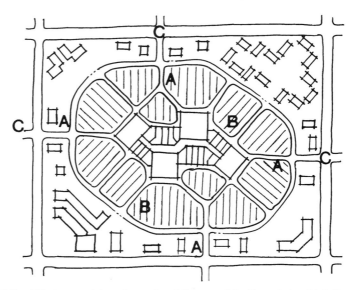

**Sketch 7.7** (**A**) Access drives from the obligatory "ring" road should define parking areas of no more than 800 cars, and should be heavily landscaped to create a sense of enclosure for the individual parking areas. (**B**) All parking should orient to the building to psychologically shorten the distances, to ease pedestrian access, and to enhance surveillance opportunities. (**C**) Primary vehicle entry-points to mall should be in the vicinity of the major anchor stores.

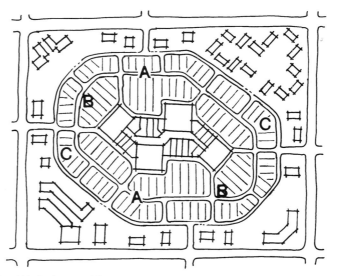

**Sketch 7.8** (**A**) A ring road located at the functional 300-foot distance from the mall entrances would contain all the required parking for the vast majority of the time. (**B**) The internal ring road and its associated landscaping help reduce the size and scale of the parking lot. (**C**) The parcels created between the ring roads become excellent opportunities for infill development, particularly offices, as they provide daytime customers for the mall as well as nighttime and weekend parking.

stops that occur with one shopping trip; thus, no overlapping of parking requirements is even considered.

- Most regional commercial sites are now required to provide between five and five-and-a-half spaces per 1000 square feet of gross leasable space, or enough to satisfy all but the peak 10 hours during the course of the year. If we assume that most commercial space is open for 12 hours a day, six days a week, then the parking areas of these commercial sites are full only 0.25 percent of the time or less. Said another way, 99.75 percent of the time the parking lot is not full and is being underutilized. This expanse of unused asphalt is unattractive at best, appalling at worst. Designing parking areas that will be fully utilized for such a short period of time throughout the year is a waste of potential commercial space and the tax receipts that could be generated if it were developed. It is also an affront to the environment, considering the heat gain to the ambient air from solar reflection and the increased surface drainage and pollution from overpaving.

- The large parking areas required by ordinance that surround all regional commercial sites have become modern-day moats, literally cutting off any normal pedestrian interaction with the commercial structure.

- Security has become a major issue in the parking areas surrounding regional centers. These seas of parking leave one feeling exposed and vulnerable and have made shoppers easy targets for crime. It is interesting to note that this particular type of crime, whether real or potential, is one of the major factors that contributed to the atrophy of our cities' older, stagnant shopping districts.

## An Alternative Future

Of all that can be said about our suburban commercial districts, one thing stands true: Americans are in a deep love/hate relationship with them. We simultaneously demand the convenience they offer and are dismayed by their appearance. Writing in 1962, Kevin Lynch perhaps said it best: "In its gaudy confusion, it seems to symbolize the worst of our material culture."[10] Typical strip commercial development is universally condemned by municipal authorities and residents alike, to the point that many municipal comprehensive planning documents contain strident statements in an attempt to limit their application. Yet they persist, for they provide a service and function that we have all come to expect.

So we accept their inevitability and go about softening, screening, buffering, and separating strip development from our residential areas even more, using all manner of landscaping, fencing, and berming, rather than exploring

[10]Kevin Lynch. *Site Planning,* Second Edition, Cambridge, Mass.: M.I.T. Press, 1962.

**Figure 7.3**   Landscaping is used as a bandaid for poor design.

a different structure, a different way of designing these sites. These aesthetic bandaids are nothing more than surface remedies that do not go to the root of the problem.

Is there an alternative approach to commercial design? Can anything be done to stop this cycle of development that perpetuates itself simply because that's the way it's always been done? Possibly. But we must revisit and reassess the current commercial development patterns at five distinct levels to devise a more community oriented, pedestrian friendly, and less automobile dependent solution for each. By examining these five levels of site design: *individual sites, neighborhood centers, community centers, major intersections,* and *malls,* solutions can be found and axioms established that work at the smallest scale and can be built upon through each successive size and scale change, to arrive at a potentially new form of suburban development, one where community is more than a nice idea.

### Individual Sites

TYPICAL LAYOUT

Building placement on individual lots, also known as *outparcels* or *pad sites,* when utilized in conjunction with shopping centers, is dictated by front, side, and rear setback lines, but generally allows the placement to occur anywhere behind or within these arbitrary lines. This situation usually leads to building placement at the center or rear of the site. In the latter a substantial landscape buffer normally is required if the site is adjacent to a residential area. In both cases, however, the parking is located in front of the building, and in some cases all around the building in an effort to be as efficient as possible, given that the building normally is located 30 to 35 feet back from the right-of-way line. This approach ensures that the view from the adjacent street is always of parked automobiles and more often than not an empty parking lot. This multiple option in placement results in a variable building line or edge with one building not relating to the next, further weakening their connection with the street and any continuity between them. This point is most important, for it is this weakening of the streetscape that goes to the heart of the problem with our suburban aesthetic (see Sketch 7.9).

ALTERNATIVE LAYOUT

By requiring that buildings be located at a *reduced setback line,* many positive things can happen. It encourages the parking to be located at the side and rear of the building and screens the parked cars from the street. Locating the building closer to the street creates a more human-scale streetscape while encouraging the development of a usable exterior public space in the form of a plaza, bus stop, outside eating area, and so on. This also reduces the need

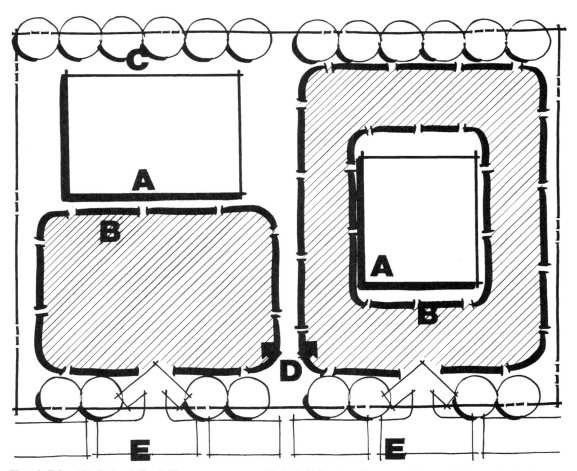

**Sketch 7.9** (**A**) Setback flexibility encourages multiple building locations, creating confusion and chaotic conditions. (**B**) Setback requirement forces parking in front of building, reducing ability to connect to street, weakening pedestrian environment. (**C**) Rear building location requires extensive landscaping when adjacent to residential and eliminates potential for pedestrian access. (**D**) Parked cars dominate view. (**E**) Flexible curb-cut location can result in confusion and aggravate traffic. (*Courtesy of the Talbot Group*)

for freestanding signs, which, by the way, can now be affixed to the building and designed as part of the structure itself. This practice alone can greatly improve the suburban visual environment (see Sketch 7.10).

In the case of areas where there is a potential for shallow strip commercial development, this approach can aid in establishing an orderly arrangement of parking lot entrances, thus enhancing the safety of the street. An added advantage of this street-oriented approach is that it shifts the vehicular access

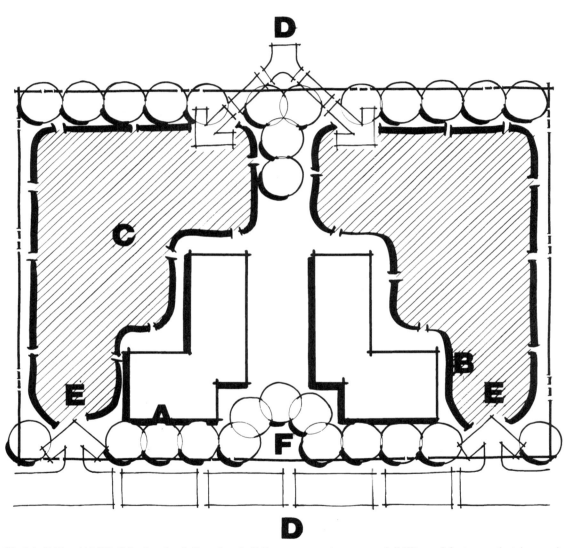

**Sketch 7.10**　(**A**) "*Build to*" setback line sites building at street; increases visibility and fosters pedestrian environment. (**B**) Parking at or behind building line maintains street "edge," draws attention to building. (**C**) Views of parked cars reduced by building location. (**D**) Neighborhood access encouraged by street-oriented building location. (**E**) Parking access separated to maximum extent and combined with adjacent parcel when applicable. (**F**) Usable exterior public space possible—artwork, fountain, bus stop, outdoor dining. (*Courtesy of the Talbot Group*)

**Figure 7.4** Parking should be located at the side and rear...

**Figure 7.5** ...in order to create human-scaled streetscapes in front.

between and across parcels to the rear of the site, reducing the points of conflict at the entrances and allowing a more structured access from the rear, be it a larger parking lot or a residential area.

It should be noted that in this example and in those that follow both typical and alternative scenarios are drawn at the same scale and attempt to depict graphically the same buildings and parking areas. These basic design premises, while seeming simplistic, are universal in that they can and should be applied to larger shopping centers or any other commercial areas.

### Neighborhood Commercial Centers

TYPICAL LAYOUT

These 5- to 15-acre sites, located on virtually every major corner of our urban and suburban areas, simultaneously symbolize both progress and sprawl. These centers are typified by a major and minor anchor, normally a grocery store, pharmacy, a spattering of smaller shops and restaurants, and most often are sited along their rear and/or side property lines. The void between the building and the street is then filled with a parking lot, which, as in the case of the individual sites, destroys any viable pedestrian-friendly connection with the street and thus discourages its casual use. The fact that these areas usually are no more than one-third filled at any time points to the need to reexamine our parking space-to-building area requirements. It seems ludicrous to require such a high number of spaces that will be fully utilized only three to four days a year at most (see Sketch 7.11).

Typically, these structures are linear in arrangement, stretching from one corner of the site to another, discouraging a casual, browsing kind of shopping. In fact their orientation seems to encourage shoppers to make multiple parking stops throughout the length of the center—in other words, driving from store to store instead of walking. An overabundance of parking, an overwhelming scale, and a lack of visual stimulation all combine to virtually ensure that a shopper is never going to be very far from his or her means of

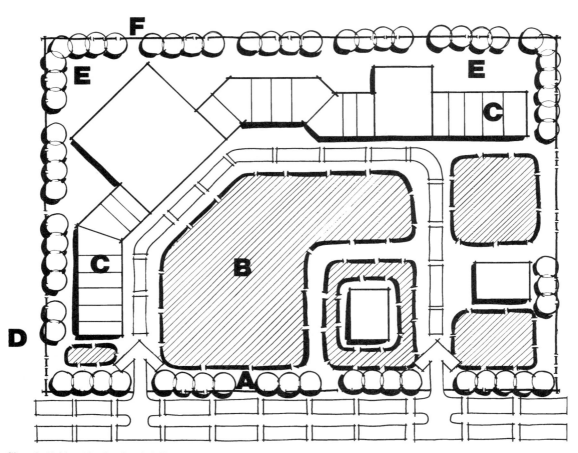

**Sketch 7.11** (**A**) Lack of defined street edge discourages pedestrian access. (**B**) Primary view is of parking area, usually half empty. (**C**) Linear arrangement does not encourage multiple shopping stops. (**D**) Limited opportunity to connect to adjacent office/commercial. (**E**) Service area too expansive; underutilized, requires heavy landscape screening. (**F**) Layout eliminates any opportunity to connect to adjacent residential area. (*Courtesy of the Talbot Group*)

private transportation. This arrangement literally requires the center to turn its back on whatever land use occurs behind it, usually residential.

This physical and psychological separation is fully achieved by locating an expansive and grossly underutilized service area that requires ever more landscaping bandaids to ameliorate its negative impact on the neighborhood. This orientation requires the adjacent residents to access their shopping center via an off-site collector road system, mixing local traffic with through traffic, and thereby exacerbating traffic congestion.

ALTERNATIVE LAYOUT

Using the same concepts established in the individual sites section, a portion of the shops can be located closer to the street, creating that desirable street edge so painfully lacking in most neighborhood centers. The main parking area can then be centralized, allowing those street-oriented shops to screen most of it from the roadway. This also encourages the scattering of smaller parking areas throughout the site, reducing their visual impact. By locating anchor stores along side property lines or back-to-back with adjacent commercial buildings, the service areas can be reduced in size, freeing space for either additional building or amenity space, and can be internalized thereby reducing the off-site visual impact. This puts the anchor stores adjacent to the bulk of the parking, where there is a true need for it (see Sketch 7.12a).

This arrangement also opens the site for the residents of adjacent housing to access the site via an internal road system, keeping local traffic separate from through traffic. In fact, additional, reduced-cost commercial frontage for smaller, neighborhood-dependent shops is created while maintaining visibility to the anchor stores from both the residential side and the primary street. The resultant *village type* commercial area, with its inward orientation and reduced spacing between buildings, encourages more shopping per trip,

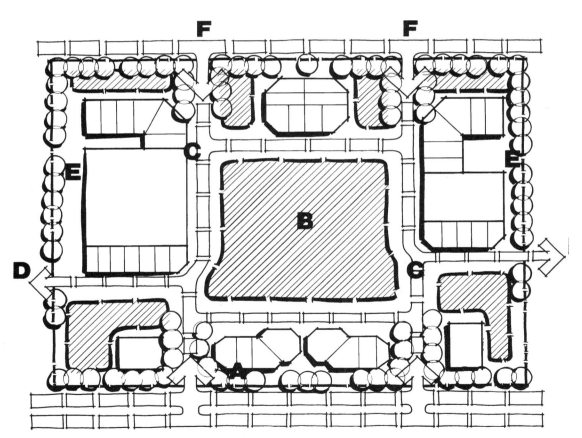

**Sketch 7.12a** (**A**) Defined street edge creates more desirable pedestrian environment. (**B**) Internal parking reduces negative impact from street. (**C**) Inward-focused arrangement creates a "village" feeling, encourages multiple shopping stops. (**D**) Strong connection to adjacent office/commercial areas. (**E**) Service areas reduced, oriented to adjacent office/commercial, less screening required. (**F**) Layout encourages use by adjacent residential, eliminating need to access via collector road system. (*Courtesy of the Talbot Group*)

**Figure 7.6**    A village commercial ambiance.

increases the efficiency of the neighborhood layout, and helps to make shopping an event to be enjoyed.

## ADAPTIVE LAYOUT

Because it is ubiquitous throughout suburbia, the neighborhood shopping center represents one of the best opportunities for adaptive reuse and integration (see Sketch 7.12b) into the fabric of the community. By simply extending streets from the surrounding residential areas into the commercial site, an entirely different relationship between the two use-areas can develop; they can become interdependent and supportive of one another. It is relatively easy to eliminate the appropriate portions of the building and replace them on-site to allow these street extensions to occur. When coupled with a realistic recognition of standard parking needs which, when considered, will reduce the number of spaces required, the result will be that additional commercial space is possible.

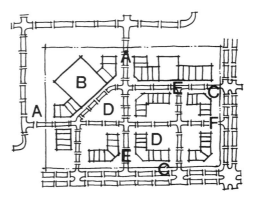

**Sketch 7.12b**    Neighborhood centers—adaptive layout. (**A**) Street extensions into commercial site; encourages local access without impacting the collector streets. (**B**) Anchor store, usually a grocery, maintains adequate parking in front. (**C**) Street edge along local collector streets is reestablished. (**D**) Bulk of shopping center parking is screened from local collector streets. (**E**) Streetscape image extends into site. (**F**) Additional accessways distribute and dilute traffic impact.

As the graphic implies, with a street orientation of shops possessing both rear-of-the-building parking and on-street parking, a transformation of these waste spaces into productive places of neighborhood activity can be achieved. In addition, with strong street connections to the surrounding neighborhood, a reduction in traffic on the local collector streets can be realized.

While this approach is certainly viable and preferable to the typical situation, it is no replacement for designing these most basic of commercial areas as part of the neighborhood from the beginning.

## Community Centers

### TYPICAL LAYOUT

These 20- to 25-acre sites are just larger versions of the neighborhood centers with more of everything—more anchors, more outparcels, more parking, and more problems. They usually are located at larger intersections and sometimes, as in the example, span the entire distance between the intersections. With a full complement of out-parcels, curb cuts, and access lanes, chaos and confusion is the norm. Again there is a weak street relationship, an overabundance of parking, and, because of their distance from the street and outparcel structures, surprisingly little visibility for the anchor stores and primary shops. Being anywhere from 400 to 800 feet away from the primary thoroughfare seems to preclude the idea of visibility so staunchly advocated by the commercial real estate brokers. Of course, in this case there is also the expansive service area that must be sealed off from the adjacent residential and screened with more "bandaids." More seriously, though, with the larger size of the center, the specter of crime and violence in these service areas becomes a major concern (see Sketch 7.13).

Finally, while in some cases there are *office centers* located adjacent or nearby, rarely are they designed to function together as a true node; more likely they are located just far enough away to require auto access between the two, resulting in more traffic, and less pedestrian interaction.

### ALTERNATIVE LAYOUT

The size and scale of community centers allows much more flexibility and creativity than is ever attempted in a typical situation. With a little innovative site manipulation, the various elements can truly be pulled together to function as a center and focus of the community and not just the community shopping center. Again, using the premises established previously, the anchor stores can be relocated closer to the intersections, actually increasing their visibility while reducing the visual impact of their parking areas. Including office sites at the corners, which in itself greatly improves the aesthetics of the site by providing something other than the typical *franchise architecture,* opportunities for overlap parking can be explored and so further reduce the need for underutilized parking areas. Also, this higher form of architecture at this location serves to anchor and give significance to the corners, establish-

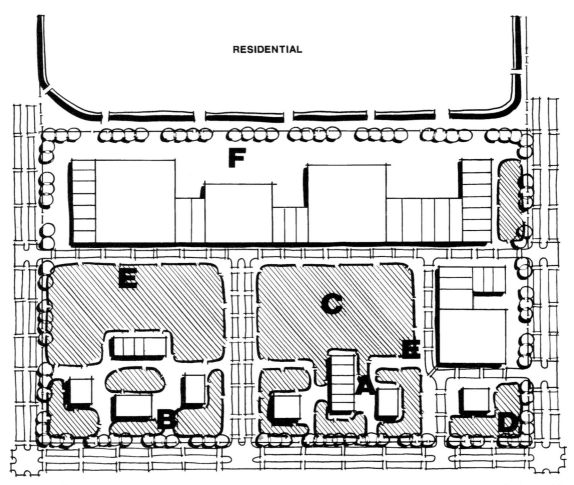

RESIDENTIAL

**Sketch 7.13** (**A**) Multiple outparcels and freestanding shops compete for attention and create confusing traffic patterns. (**B**) Parking between building and street eliminates a viable pedestrian environment. (**C**) Outparcels reduce visibility of parking area and of storefronts as well. (**D**) Parking location weakens intersection visually. A missed opportunity for public space. (**E**) Expanse of parking and size of center discourage pedestrian access across site. (**F**) Expansive service area creates underutilized paved area that requires screening and security while eliminating direct pedestrian or vehicle access to center. (*Courtesy of the Talbot Group*)

ing a stronger sense of place in an area typically weak in urban form. In addition, the inclusion of significant office space on site creates a built-in demand for commercial services and reduces the number of noontime automobile trips in the immediate vicinity, since theoretically most of the desired shopping is available on site (see Sketch 7.14).

To encourage a stronger internal pedestrian and vehicular access, the secondary shops (those that survive as a result of spin-off from the anchor stores) can potentially be configured, much like an enclosed mall, as a functional "Main Street"; this will allow both vehicular and pedestrian access, enhance the shopping experience, and encourage noontime and after-work

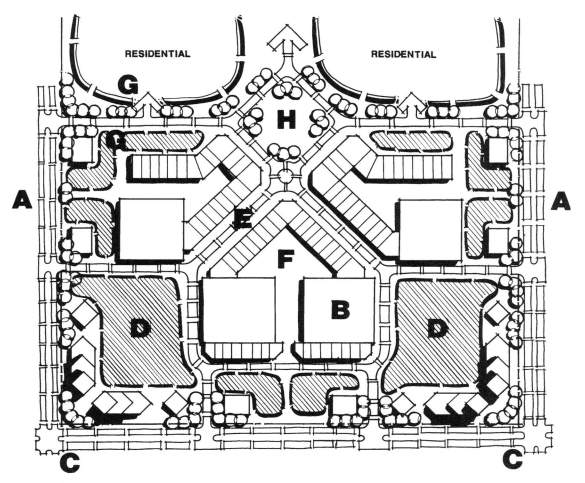

**Sketch 7.14** (**A**) Separation of outparcels reduces confusion and orientation reinforces streetscape. (**B**) Anchor stores' visibility remains the same, if not better. (**C**) Offices at intersection screen parking and foster public use of space. (**D**) Parking areas separated to reduce expansiveness and provide overlap opportunities. (**E**) "Main Street" with sidewalks and parallel parking re-creates hometown feeling, reinforces neighborhood identity, and encourages pedestrian activity. (**F**) Service areas consolidated, internalized, and controlled for security. (*G*) Access road serves both commercial and adjacent residential. (*H*) "Village green" as focal point/gathering area. (*Courtesy of the Talbot Group*)

visits by the office workers. Small-scale shops and offices and neighborhood-support commercial businesses that don't need to be seen as much from through traffic can be located at the rear of the site along a local residential access road. With *residential* fronting on one side of this road and *neighborhood commercial* on the other, a true *town commons* or some other appropriate community focal point can be established at the heart of the interface of these two seemingly disparate uses. A nice by-product of this configuration is the ability to consolidate, internalize, and control access to the commercial service areas, making them both safer and less obtrusive in the landscape.

**Figure 7.7** A truly functional "Main Street" provides for both the pedestrian and the automobile.

*Major Intersections*

TYPICAL LAYOUT

*Major intersections* are the prime community and subregional commercial locations found in every suburban growth area. Historically, they have evolved over a longer period of time than individual sites or neighborhood centers and therefore have had little benefit from long-range planning or a guided vision for the immediate area surrounding it. As Sketch 7.15 depicts, they are usually a combination of all the previous examples, more or less haphazardly strewn about randomly. Not much more can be said about these situations that hasn't been covered already, except that in most cases areawide circulation among the various commercial, office, and residential uses is channeled to and through one primary intersection. The resultant traffic is barely manageable at best, and absolutely unbearable at peak demand. The ever-increasing traffic requires more and more intersection "improvements" until what is realized is the all too familiar intersection consisting of at least eight lanes at each leg. This in effect separates one side of the road from the other, to the extent that there is little, if any, normal pedestrian access possible from one to the other. Oh yes, the stop bars are there for automobiles, the striping, signage, and signals are there for the pedestrian, but are there any pedestrians? Rarely! The scale of these intersections is so vast that a person actually walking across them seems odd and out of place. To see a person on foot here makes the passing motorist assume he or she is having car trouble and is obviously headed to one of the automotive service centers located on each of the four primary corners. Obviously we jest, but it's easy to understand how in our attempt to solve problems we can actually destroy the underlying desirability of a place, thereby cancelling out the need for the improvements (see Sketch 7.15).

The scattered and unfocused development along these major roads represents one of the inherent faults of the totally laissez faire approach to physical planning by our municipal authorities. The missed opportunities at these criti-

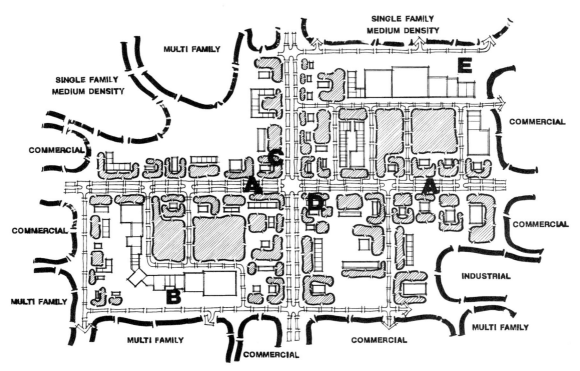

**Sketch 7.15** (**A**) Multiple sites and curb cuts create confusion, visual clutter, traffic congestion, and weak streetscape. (**B**) Service areas exposed to residential discourage pedestrian access via main collector roads. (**C**) Most local and through traffic concentrates at one intersection. (**D**) No opportunity for urban amenity, community focal points. (**E**) Existing pattern encourages continuation of current development. (*Courtesy of the Talbot Group*)

cal points, opportunities to create a synergy, a focus, a true sense of place, will take a generation or more to correct.

ALTERNATIVE LAYOUT

Using similar patterns to those described for the community centers and clustering them to focus on the four corners of the intersection, a unifying order and structure can be achieved while all the services and land uses one would expect are provided. Elimination of the individual curb cuts for the freestanding buildings and outparcels along the primary thoroughfares reduces the *friction* so hated by transportation engineers. Instead, these outparcels can be clustered between median breaks and access granted using cross-easements along the rear of their properties. These critically located median breaks can be positioned to siphon off the local commercial traffic at eight points on the primary roads, to feed the traffic into two circular collector loops that, in essence, circle the primary intersection. This separation of traffic then allows freer, less-impeded movement of through traffic at the primary intersection and encourages commercial locations between the two loop roads. In addition, it creates an easier transition to the various residential areas outside the loop roads, so that a community circulation system separates the commercial from the residential, and not the barren service area as is so typically the case. In effect, this, then, becomes the neighborhood commercial street, directly accessible to the residential areas without requiring access via a major thoroughfare. Major anchor stores serviced by the inner circulation loop retain good visibility and access while minor anchor stores, primarily neighborhood support, can be accessed from the outer circulation loop with orientation toward the very residential areas they serve (see Sketch 7.16).

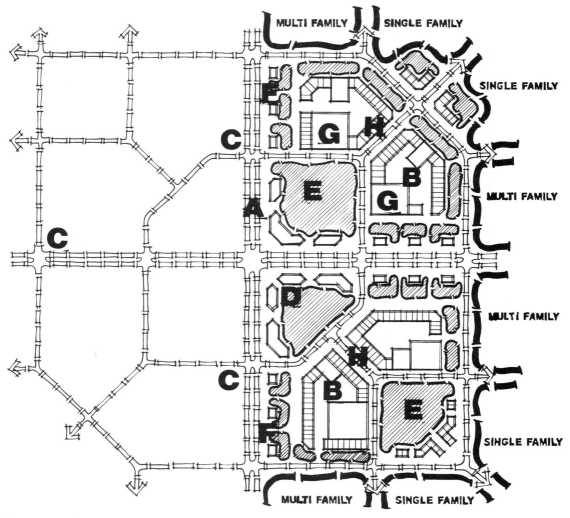

**Sketch 7.16** (**A**) No curb cuts between median breaks; allows easy movement of through traffic. (**B**) Combined internalized service areas are more efficient and controllable, and eliminate need for screening. (**C**) Multiple access points siphon local traffic from through traffic. (**D**) Multistory corporate offices at primary intersection; creates continuous street edge, enhancing pedestrian activity. (**E**) Primary parking areas screened from traffic provide overlap possibilities. (**F**) Outparcels clustered to support offices and shops while retaining visibility, shared entrances. (*G*) Anchor stores retain same or better visibility. (*H*) Neighborhood "Main Street" centrally located to support offices and residential. (*Courtesy of the Talbot Group*)

With the commercial area forming a "doughnut," if you will, around the primary intersection, this core area is then freed for the location of multistoried offices clustered adjacent to the intersection. Located in this manner to screen the parking areas and enhance the pedestrian activity in the area, the result is an office and commercial district that is a true part of the community. In fact, it would form, and function as, the heart of the community.

The alternative concepts discussed previously are certainly appropriate in this situation. Overlap parking between the office areas (daytime during-the-week users) and the commercial areas (nighttime during-the-week and weekend users) increases site efficiency. Screened, centralized service areas enhance safety and reduce the negative visual environment. Neighborhood "Main Streets" reinforce community identity while providing an alternative shopping experience. Obviously this type of treatment could not and probably should not be applied at every intersection. A better application would be to develop in noncommercial fashion a few more intersections while consolidating a district's support commercial area in fewer areas. For this reason this special, focused approach is more effective when utilized sparingly, both because of the size of the area required to support it residentially and the desirability of creating a few truly distinct nodal areas that can be easily recognized as the center of a geographic region.

## Malls

### TYPICAL LAYOUT

*Malls,* the modern-day downtowns of suburban America, are in many cases regional and superregional centers that can easily exceed 150 or 200 acres in size and be located in their own isolated, extremely large superblock. Ideally they are bordered by collector roads with relatively quick access to a limited access highway. Originally they consisted of the mall site only, but now they have evolved to the point of being surrounded by numerous transitional and support facilities. Such facilities may include neighborhood or community shopping centers, individual office sites and entire office developments, hotels, freestanding restaurants, automobile maintenance facilities, and medium- to high-density residential, all requiring separate, individual parking areas. These facilities tend to form a continuous, seemingly protective zone around the centrally located mall structure, from which, however, they are completely separated by the giant parking lot (see Sketch 7.17).

The primary organizing element in this scenario is the *ring road,* which forms the outer limits of the mall site. Other than the occasional retention area or landscape island, nothing but asphalt occurs from this point to the mall itself; in some cases this is only a couple of hundred feet, but more often than not can easily be 600 to 800 feet or more. The purpose, obviously, is to provide adequate on-site circulation from the ancillary uses, but when riding this ring road in our quest to find the perfectly situated parking space we

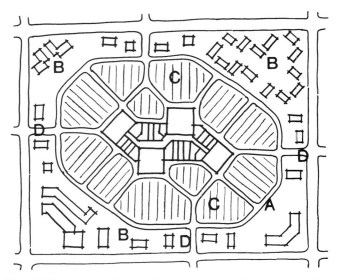

**Sketch 7.17** (**A**) The ring road typically serves as the primary organizing element of the entire area. (**B**) A variety of related but unconnected uses such as restaurants, banks, offices, additional retail, and even residential surround the mall. (**C**) A massive parking lot usually separates the mall and its surrounding support structures. (**D**) Access to the surrounding road network is channelized and focused at only a few points, requiring signalization and exacerbating traffic flow.

resemble the little white ball on a roulette wheel, circling till we plunge inward to the center to find our resting spot.

This complex is linked to the area collector roads via several short entrance roads that serve as extensions of the local road system. This is typically the only feigned attempt to integrate these facilities with the surrounding community. In fact, most often heavy landscape screening and buffering is mandated for site plan approval, so as to reduce the negative impact of such a monolithic and obviously out-of-scale structure.

The design intent of the relationship between the mall structure and its parking seems in conflict with the true purpose of the structure itself. The mall is designed to pull people in, primarily through prominently located and architecturally accented anchor stores. These command the premier positions with the most visibility and are located as far away from one another as the design will permit. The secondary entrances, those leading directly to the smaller mall shops, are likely to be understated to discourage access. However, these smaller shops form the filler between the anchors, and through interesting design, promotional activities, seasonal displays, and so on, customers are enticed to walk past them in the hope that an article or piece of clothing will catch their eye and prompt a sale. The question is, if access through the anchors is preferred, why provide such an abundance of parking all around? Why not provide most of the required parking in the vicinity of the anchors only and utilize the other parking areas more productively: office, hotel, or, heaven forbid, high-density housing in the form of apartments, or housing for the elderly.

With the exception of the hotel and what little residential may be on site, the vast majority of the uses are the 8 a.m. to 5 p.m. offices and the 9 a.m. to 9 p.m. commercial spaces. This means that for nearly 50 percent of the day this sea of asphalt stands empty.

## ALTERNATIVE LAYOUT

The automobile gives reason to the necessity of malls. Malls exist only because cars do, and cars are needed because most people don't live or work near a mall, and to go from one place to another they need large, streamlined, superelevated, limited-access roads. These, in turn, allow people to live farther and farther out, requiring more roads, which eventually leads to the need for another mall site. The cycle continues.

With the problems that growth and development are creating—overburdened infrastructure and residents, lack of community attachment, polarization of various socioeconomic groups, and stress on the environment—a new pattern must be identified to accommodate societal needs. Malls are the *climax species* of the commercial genre, the culmination of a merchandising concept begun in the first half of the twentieth century which many feel is destined to and *must* mutate to another form that will be more accommodating to the shopper than to the automobile.

The commercial district of our suburban areas must be woven back into the fabric of the community by reestablishing a street orientation for the structures, and, through a realistic accounting of the parking requirements, relegating the automobile and its storage facility, the parking lot, to a subjugated, secondary role. The *box in a lot* mentality of site planning must be eliminated and replaced with the more street-oriented approach we have been discussing. Mall sites and their ancillary land uses should be developed as continuations of the immediate area and not the isolated superblocks they are today. Entrance roads and ring roads should be configured as true extensions of the local street system, allowing direct access from the surrounding area and reducing traffic on the local collector streets (see Sketch 7.18).

As the example suggests, we need to first identify how existing mall sites can be adapted to provide additional street-oriented uses such as offices, commercial, residential, even warehouse/distribution operations, all within the immediate area. Secondly, we need to design future mall sites with the idea that they will serve as the first phase or core of an eventual street-oriented mixed-use development.

If the ancillary support structures are developed using the design concepts stressed in previous portions of this chapter, what once were just mall sites could emerge as new suburban centers of shopping, social, and civic activities set in a radically different form from the isolated asphalt deserts we all know, but not so different from time-tested, tried and true solutions evident in memorable places the world over.

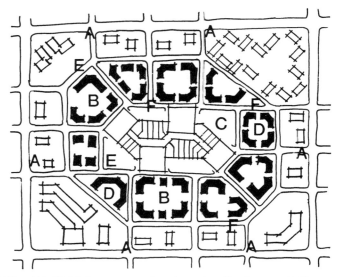

**Sketch 7.18** (**A**) Multiple access points into site distribute and dilute traffic. (**B**) New development can easily occur between the ring road and the mall proper. Offices, street-oriented shops, and high-density residential are ideal complementary uses. (**C**) Realistic requirements reduce the need for an overabundance of parking spaces. (**D**) Parking at the rear of the new structures is screened from casual view from the new "streets." (**E**) Surface and/or structured parking can be accommodated and afforded with the increased revenues resulting from the additional development. (**F**) Walkable streetscape reduces the perceived scale of the site and encourages pedestrian access.

# CHAPTER 8

# Where We Work

Where community residents choose to work is a personal choice that depends on any number of factors including education, skill, training, and personal choice. Although there are countless places where people can work in the community, our primary focus here will be the suburban office park. While it is true that office parks account for only a portion of jobs, it is the office park that typifies suburban development, with commercial and retail businesses acting in a supporting role.

## Suburban Office Parks

Most suburban office parks are one of three styles: *campus*, *urban villages*, or *freestanding* independent structures. With parcel sizes ranging from 5 to 25 acres in size and possessing generous (50- to 100-foot) setbacks from adjacent roads and property lines, suburban office parks consume as much as *30 times* the land area per employee than that of offices located in the central business district (CBD). This is in large part due to the low-rise nature of the buildings as well as the on-site parking required for these typically remote sites. Successful parks require several features nearby: affordable housing, recreational and cultural facilities, a college, university, or even a strong technical school; and support services such as commercial, hotels, day care, restaurants, and so on. Initially, practically the only form of office structure outside the CBD, freestanding independent structures, typically located along the road out of town, are now the exception, not the rule (Figure 8.1).

**Figure 8.1**  Freestanding independent office structures, the "box in a lot."

### Campus-Style Development

This is currently the predominant choice of most developers and tenants alike. This form is typified by low-rise, large-footprint structures spaciously separated from other office buildings by generous landscaping and equally generous parking lots. The more sophisticated developments maintain a design theme with regard to architectural style, signage, and landscaping, with covenants and restrictions to govern compliance.

Covenants and restrictions (C&Rs) address a wide range of criteria to ensure that a standard of excellence is established and maintained. They set standards for such items as setbacks, landscaping, parking requirements, permitted and restricted uses, acceptable building materials, site coverage, and so on. Generally, the developments with the stricter C&Rs are perceived to be the better-designed parks, which exhibit a higher level of continuity and context. They are intended to supplement, not replace, local ordinances and can help assuage the fears of local residents concerning impact to surrounding residential areas.

While the restrictions do not ensure a better product than that which might occur if left unrestricted, the result is usually just more landscaping, wider setbacks, and more open space to functionally screen higher-intensity uses from lower-intensity ones. This, in effect, requires more land area to accommodate the same amount of building square footage, requiring more street to be built, larger parcels farther from existing development, increased commuter distances, and the elimination of any hope of mass transit access; but it does not address the basic site-design problems that prompted the need for the restrictions in the first place.

### Urban Villages

More recent phenomena are *urban villages* or *edge cities,* two names for essentially the same thing. Increasing land and development costs in these areas have resulted in the typical campus-style development going vertical, giving us a clustering of relatively tall office and apartment/condominium structures knitted together with a fabric of access roads, parking garages, and surface parking lots. Neither truly urban nor suburban, these centers rival many core cities in terms of square footage and office workers.

In large part they *evolved* rather than being *planned*. Originally, most were minor crossroads on the outskirts of town. As residential development engulfed them and the time spent commuting to the urban core became untenable, land prices rose, making vertically oriented office, commercial, and residential development cost-effective. However, most were and are being developed using the campus-style design approach. This box-in-a-lot form of freestanding building, situated in an expansive parking lot, makes little or no attempt to address or respect the street, much less other buildings adjacent to it.

## Current Design Trends

The trend for the last 40 years has been to build suburban office parks on the fringe of urbanized areas. Closer to the developing residential neighborhoods, the suburban sites offered shorter commutes during a period when interstate freeways were either nonexistent or inadequate for the volume of traffic generated daily.

Subsequent to the development of the interstate system, the suburb-to-suburb commuter trips far outnumber the suburb-to-CBD trips of decades past. With entire regions of the suburban fringe opened for increased office park activity, particularly at the interchange locations, the pristine parcels offered for both speculation office sites and corporate headquarters boast *location* and *access,* which rank as perhaps the two most important criteria, with *proximity* to all modes of transportation being extremely important to marketability. And as an added bonus, the *visibility* afforded by this location is not only appealing to corporate clients and the architects of the buildings, the proximity allows employees to live closer to their place of employment and to spend less time on the road.

Despite their seeming benefits, the freeway orientation has led to the development of suburban office parks as enclaves separate from the neighborhoods they were to serve. While boasting proximity, they are rarely tied directly to residential areas, forcing a reliance on the automobile for practically all access. Their low-density development design prohibits any real effort to serve the sites with mass transit unless a large mall is located nearby. Today, the increasing demand for sites farther and farther removed from the developed areas requires greater dependence on the automobile for access and increasingly longer reverse commutes for employees.

## Typical Problems with Not-So-Typical Solutions

### TYPICAL

- Too often diversification of land use is sacrificed to create a homogeneous physical environment for all the parcels within the development. Parks typ-

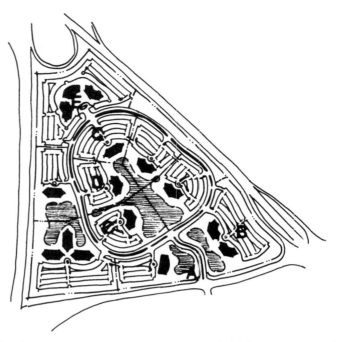

**Sketch 8.1** Campus-style office development. (**A**) Divided entrance through amenity lakes sets the tone and theme of the development. (**B**) Parking orientation requires walking between the parked cars, creating awkward access and an unsafe situation. (**C**) Massive surface parking lots usually overwhelm and obliterate the site. (**D**) "Box-in-a-lot" configuration discourages interaction between office buildings. (**E**) The prime office parcel has the worst access.

ically are designed to provide a limited range of parcel sizes to prospective businesses in the interest of creating similarity of land uses and site design; so much so that one office parks looks essentially like every other. In addition, this exclusion of certain uses limits site sales, inevitably increasing the time required to complete it (see Sketch 8.1).

*ALTERNATIVE*

- Incorporate a number of land uses within the framework of the park (see Sketch 8.2). These should not just be located within the park boundaries but should be intimately tied to the office areas with common street access. Commercial, high-density residential, industrial, yes, even single-family residential, can all be considered acceptable and compatible uses within a well-designed park. The potential to live and work close by is becoming more appealing to a larger segment of society. Reduced traffic and commutation times, more efficient land use, greater security through the presence of people throughout the day, to say nothing of the reduced build-out time, are just a few of the benefits of this approach to site design. While it is true that there is no current relationship of workers living near their place of work, it still stands to reason to provide residential and commercial areas

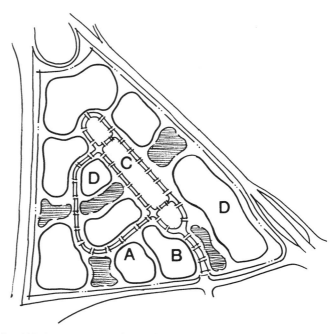

**Sketch 8.2** (**A**) Apartments and townhomes provide on-site housing opportunities and spread the development risk. (**B**) Commercial situated to support offices and on-site residential whole, capturing drive-by trips. (**C**) Central greenspace/park provides visible access to premier office site, which now becomes the park focal point. (**D**) Combination of parcels is possible to provide a variety of site sizes and uses, thereby enhancing the park's marketability.

within easy access of one another. Offices need supplies and support services, workers need a place for lunch and quick shopping during the noon hour and after work, the residents need convenient opportunities for professional services offered by doctors, lawyers, insurance agents, and so forth. The commercial area needs a standing daytime and evening population to survive. All uses need and depend on each other and are better and more successful for their being close to one another. In fact, if all three uses are located say, within one-quarter to one-half mile of one another, we might even see people using the sidewalks.

*TYPICAL*

- Suburban office parks are nothing more than large subdivisions. Rights-of-way of 50 to 60 feet create frontage for parcels for sale and development. This approach to land subdivision may be appropriate for residential, but it leads to the typical box-in-a-lot site design for office parks. Buildings are placed in the center of a large parking lot, physically and psychologically separated from one another, with little or no inducement to encourage pedestrian access between them. Indeed, rarely is there any direct vehicular access possible between them. Some major corporate headquarters offer an extreme example of this. Located miles from other office centers and sur-

**Figure 8.2**   Cluster design. (*Courtesy of CMSS Architects*)

rounded by acres of forest in large part to satisfy the whims of the CEO, they reinforce the philosophy of aloofness and disdain for our urban and suburban areas. It seems ludicrous to create such introverted office development so far removed from any other, having no contact with any other offices or even commercial for that matter. Many of these headquarters, under the guise of environmental sensitivity, require thousands of employees to drive extremely long distances through countryside, only to arrive at a parking garage (see Sketches 8.3 and 8.4).

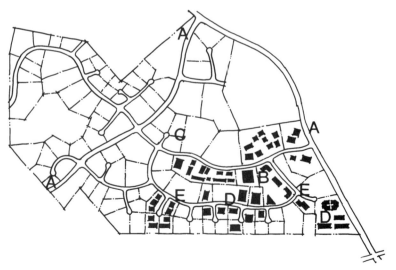

**Sketch 8.3**   (**A**) No clearly defined entrance announces the beginning of the development. (**B**) Random placement of buildings, varied building sizes, and arbitrary parcel sizes create a sense of chaos and disorder. (**C**) Uncelebrated center robs the development of a potential focal point or orientation element. (**D**) The lack of a definite street edge erodes overall continuity of the park. (**E**) Double and triple frontage lots reduce the efficiency of the park layout.

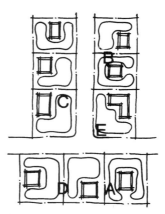

**Sketch 8.4** (**A**) No sense of connection or continuity between parcels due to the varied placement of buildings. (**B**) Varied and uncoordinated setbacks create a "ragged edge" quality to the streetscape. (**C**) Little, if any, physical connection between parking areas. (**D**) Distance between buildings and paved environment discourages pedestrian access and interaction. (**E**) Typical view from the street is primarily of pavement.

*ALTERNATIVE*

- Encourage building placements toward the street and toward one another to create relationships between buildings and the street (see Sketch 8.5). Rather than creating stand-alone icons to our egos or to our architects, we should look for opportunities to tie structures together, to establish a context of design, a continuity of place. This will greatly enhance the off-site image of the park by drawing attention to the buildings and not the parking lots, landscaping, and signage. Who knows, if we were to follow this approach we might even achieve something resembling a streetscape in our suburban office parks (see Sketch 8.6).

- In more intensely developed areas we should utilize building locations to anchor the corners and provide access to the internal parking areas away from the corner and preferably combined with the entrance to another office site. This would enhance the street aesthetics by reducing curb cuts while screening the cars.

*TYPICAL*

- Most developers overbuild their parking areas to make them more marketable. They feel that the availability of additional parking enhances their chances of leasing the property faster. The result is underutilized parking areas, and overpaved sites, which increases surface runoff and degrades the environment, and results in visually unappealing areas. This is aggravated by the municipalities in that all required parking must be provided on-site with no allowances for on-street parking.

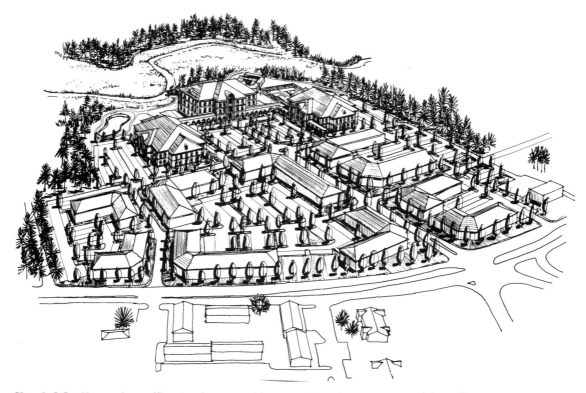

**Sketch 8.5** Harmonious office development with street orientation. (*Courtesy of the Talbot Group*)

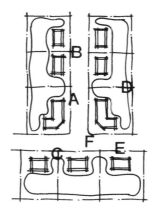

**Sketch 8.6** (**A**) Reduced setback and street orientation screens parking areas and improves street ambiance. (**B**) Close association of buildings encourages interaction between them. (**C**) Combined and shared points of access reduce traffic conflict and enhance safety. (**D**) Cross-access in parking lot facilitates traffic movement and reduces street traffic. (**E**) Closer proximity to street reduces need for freestanding signs. (**F**) View on street is of architecture and landscaping.

**Figure 8.3** Encourage building placement *toward* the street. (*Courtesy of CMSS Architects*)

*ALTERNATIVE*

- Municipalities should require parking only for leasable spaces within a building. Very often total building square footage is used to compute the number of parking spaces required. This includes all restrooms, maintenance areas, lobby spaces, stairwells, and hallways—spaces not associated with leasable area. Not including these spaces in the calculation could reduce the required parking by 10 to 30 percent. Municipalities should not allow any more parking than is required unless a true need is established, and definitely not without a variance being approved.

In addition, large collector roads usually provide the access for such parks and could be more efficient and productive if allowed to provide some on-street parking for the offices. This would work very well, especially if the buildings were sited toward the road and not the rear of the site, since most people are reluctant to walk more than 300 feet from their cars to their offices. On-street parking makes fiscal sense, too. Millions upon millions of tax dollars go for the construction of major roadways with their express and exclusive use as conduits from one place to another. Usually these are filled only at peak hours while the rest of the time they are somewhat underutilized. By encouraging some parking at key areas along these roads, taxpayers receive more for their money, and more land can be either set aside for green-space preservation or developed as taxable property. When one considers that each parking space costs anywhere from $1000 to $1500, it is a wonder that developers are willing to incur such an additional expense.

*TYPICAL*

- Wide collector streets that serve suburban office parks are not designed for the human scale and thus discourage pedestrian use. This is aggravated when parking is located immediately adjacent to the street and the office

**Sketch 8.7**  (**A**) Pedestrian access between opposite-facing buildings is discouraged through parking lot arrangement and location. (**B**) Office park collector street is physically removed from the buildings it serves, further discouraging pedestrian use. (**C**) As sidewalks in collector streets are surrounded by large parking areas, they go unused because space is inhospitable and unsafe. (**D**) Only two environments result from this arrangement: inside the office and the paved parking areas.

building is located to the rear of the site. In essence, the space is too open and creates an uncomfortable, vulnerable feeling in those who chose to walk in it (see Sketch 8.7).

*ALTERNATIVE*

- Encourage building locations closer to the street and parking at or behind the building setback line (see Sketch 8.8). Generally, people feel uncomfortable in wide-open spaces, especially when forced to walk adjacent to several lanes of traffic. Currently, most streets that serve suburban office parks lack any sense of enclosure similar to that described in Chapter 1. Even if there were someplace to walk to in these parks, the trip there is usually so inhospitable that few make the attempt (see Sketch 8.9).

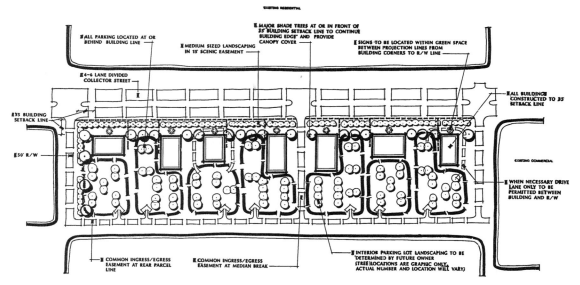

**Sketch 8.8**  Concept for office/commercial along a major roadway. (*Courtesy of the Talbot Group*)

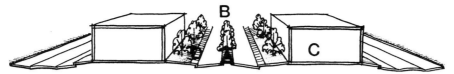

**Sketch 8.9** (**A**) A building placement adjacent to the collector street creates a sense of enclosure, thus reassuring pedestrians. (**B**) Visual accessibility between offices encourages pedestrian accessibility. (**C**) Buildings screen views of the parking areas and enhance both the vehicular and pedestrian experience. (**D**) With this arrangement, a third environment, a streetscape, is created, enriching both the space and the experience.

*TYPICAL*

- The regional thoroughfare system is a deterrent to any reasonable jobs-housing balance in a particular area. With the high-volume, high-speed road system in place in most areas, living far from our place of employment is not only possible, it is greatly encouraged. It is actually possible for someone living on the other side of town to get to work in a suburban office park faster than someone living closer but forced to use the local collector streets. Concentration of offices in just a few areas aggravates traffic regionally, requiring more and longer commuting trips. While low-density suburban office development has eased traffic within its site, it has done so at the expense of the traffic off-site (see Sketch 8.10).

*ALTERNATIVE*

- Suburban office centers should be more evenly dispersed throughout the region to provide reasonable office opportunities at the local scale. Local

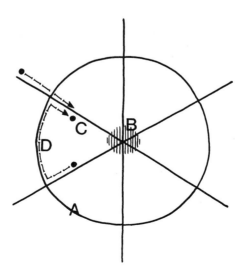

**Sketch 8.10** (**A**) Regional road network. (**B**) Downtown/central business district. (**C**) Employment center. (**D**) Although living closer to the place of employment, this resident travels farther by using the regional road network.

collector streets need to be tied to the local office clusters to provide direct access to them from the immediate neighborhoods that surround them. Besides, a trip to the office down a residentially scaled and commercially devoid local collector street can be a very pleasant experience. If given the choice, most people would opt for the local collector, or parkway, as it were. In the case of two-income families, this scenario allows and encourages at least one family member to work in the local office park and the other at a more remote site, with the latter dropping off the former at his or her place of employment (see Sketch 8.11).

*TYPICAL*

- In the rare instance where there are other land uses near a suburban office park, usually there is no attempt to incorporate them into a larger development. Instead, great pains are taken to separate each totally from one another. Most municipalities have devised elaborate landscaping, fencing, and buffering ordinances to soften the edges between seemingly disparate uses. Zoning district lines are much more than just so much ink on mylar; they are invaluable borders more important than property lines in establishing the checkerboard land-use patterns prevalent in our larger cities and suburbs. Rather than confronting the friction that exists between differing uses and arriving at a physical solution that addresses the concerns, we typ-

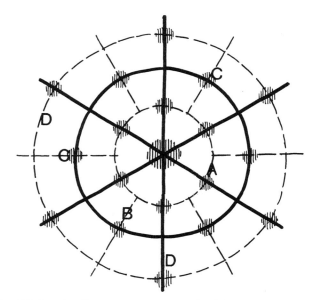

**Sketch 8.11** (**A**) Local collector street system should support and complement the regional network. (**B**) Local collectors should interconnect to allow convenient local access and provide an alternative to regional network. (**C**) Commercial/employment center is best located at the intersection points of both local and regional networks. (**D**) Radial and circumferential movement from and around the central business district should be the primary role of transportation.

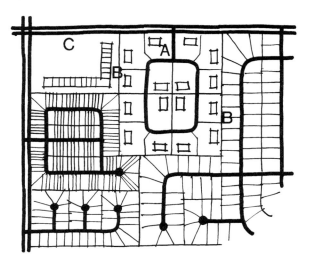

**Sketch 8.12** (**A**) Singular point of access to office park and other proximate land uses requires collector road access, restricts cross-zoning movement, and exacerbates local traffic. (**B**) Supposedly incongruent land-uses adjacent to one another require extensive setbacks, landscaping, fencing, and other buffers to force a separation between them. (**C**) Access to commercial area by local collector street only.

ically rely on the bandaids mentioned above to smooth over the conflicts (see Sketch 8.12).

*ALTERNATIVE*

- Generally, it is better design to blend one land use into another with a sensitive system of streets, building siting, and parking arrangements to provide the smooth transition between land uses. All it takes is a little design effort to articulate the elements of open space, circulation, and structure, using the methods described above to create a logical flow of uses throughout the width and breadth of our developed and developing areas. Sketch 8.13 depicts how the scenario established in Sketch 8.12 could be modified to incorporate more lines of movement between land uses. This is not an ideal situation but it does depict how access could be adapted to create stronger cross-zoning ties. In Chapter 9 we will discover how this area could have been designed to truly integrate one land use with another.

## Summary

What we are espousing here is that the areas in and around our suburban office parks be considered what they should and can be—mixed-use developments. In general, mixed-use developments offer higher land values because of the various activities present on-site for a longer period of time than conventional single-use development. The hard transition lines so prevalent

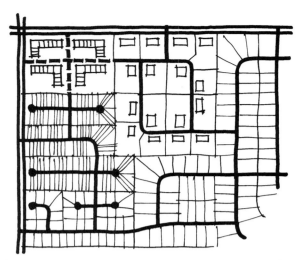

**Sketch 8.13** Indirect movement through zoning areas/land uses is encouraged by street connections.

today can and should be eliminated unless we wish to see more traffic congestion and longer commutes. We need to reverse the form of urban development unleashed with the availability of inexpensive fuel and the untethered highway construction of past decades. We need to think more of neighborhoods and less of subdivisions, more of interaction and less of screening, more of access and less of restriction; in short, more of community and less of sprawl.

CHAPTER 9

# Where We Relax:
# Our Public Sites and
# Open Spaces

## A Historical Perspective

The importance of public open spaces throughout the course of history is indisputable. Whole volumes have been written documenting the various shapes and sizes of these common meeting grounds, from the Greek agora to Central Park in New York. All previous cultures placed a high regard on these spaces and seemed to understand their significance to the well-being of their citizens. Indeed, through the nineteenth century in this country, that significance was respected. More recently, however, the role of these spaces as a civilizing element seems to have been either forgotten or neglected.

Originally these were the primary places for commercial activity, business, and politics as well as places to relax and enjoy friends and neighbors. Public places were the social hearts of the communities and as such were usually the site of the community's more significant buildings. All manner of churches, guild halls, civic buildings, and prominent dwellings were either situated in these spaces or formed an enclosure around a space. From a European perspective, the open space was the dominant element in this arrangement while the buildings, playing a minor role, simply became the vertical elements of

167

the space. These were usually totally paved; the result was a very flexible activities space, in that circulation or use areas were interchangeable. In America they were adapted to create a "green" enclosed by a street or road.

This was the predominant form of formal open space in America until Daniel Burnham and Frederick Law Olmsted collaborated on the 1893 World Columbian Exposition in Chicago. Following the premises of the popular *City Beautiful* movement of the day, they created a truly monumental city in classic style and organization, utilizing sweeping vistas, wide, parklike boulevards, grand civic buildings, and greenspaces as focal points. The roots of this movement had their beginning with the rebuilding of Paris by Napoleon III and his lieutenant Baron Haussmann—perhaps the first major effort at urban renewal.

This opening up of the city triggered a different perception of cities wherein movement into and through them became much easier and allowed ample access to the open spaces beyond their borders. However, the advent of World War I put an end to any further serious attempts at incorporating open space into the fabric of the city. What emerged from this bleak period was a pragmatism, a practicality that would not allow attention to such "frivolous" matters as beauty, ambience, and grandeur. The age of innocence was gone. The grand pedestrian boulevards were transformed into urban expressways.

In the 1950s, following two world wars and an economic depression, the concept of city structure and open space had changed. Restrictive zoning was now the primary means of giving order to a city and its burgeoning suburbs, and open space was merely the area lying between existing development and the leapfrog subdivisions popping up everywhere. The concept of parks and recreation had been separated and only active recreation in the form of ballfields and court games was being given any serious attention; usually, these were built in conjunction with the many junior high and high schools needed for the baby boom generation.

In the rush to the suburbs we had sacrificed that community unifying element that had served mankind so well for thousands of years, all in the name

**Figure 9.1**   The grand pedestrian boulevard of old...

**Figure 9.2**    ...has been transformed into the urban expressway.

of progress. Open space had become merely the leftover space in subdivisions, that area that probably couldn't be developed anyway or was situated too far from existing utilities to be considered profitable to develop as anything else. So, in the span of 30 to 35 years, community open space had gone from being on equal footing with those other two elements we discussed earlier, circulation and structure, to being subordinate to them. Note that during this same time period we experienced revolutions in traffic engineering that gave us elevated freeways, grade-separated interchanges, and limited-access highways in addition to homogenized "franchise" architecture and the incredibly impersonal and aloof architecture of the modernist movement. It might be said that these two revolutions in circulation and structure have done more to destroy the concept of community than any other two single elements combined.

## The Current Situation

It is true, however, that the last 10 to 15 years have brought a rediscovery, if you will, of center city community spaces, especially in those cities fortunate enough to possess water frontage. The unprecedented push to create or improve waterfront parks all across the nation points to the fact that people everywhere are starved for the type of interaction these modern-day agoras offer. The success of these urban parks (not recreation areas) offers hope that people have an innate desire to congregate and enjoy one another's company in a public setting and that a similar desire can be manifested in a suburban setting; for it is these types of spaces that are so sorely lacking there. In fact, one might even say that it is tacit vindication of Burnham and Olmstead in their approach to urban open space.

Currently, open space takes two forms in suburbia. The first are activity areas for organized sports like softball, tennis, swimming, soccer, and so on (see Sketch 9.1); and the other are preservation areas such as floodplains, wetlands, steep-slope areas, drainage channels, and so forth. The former are

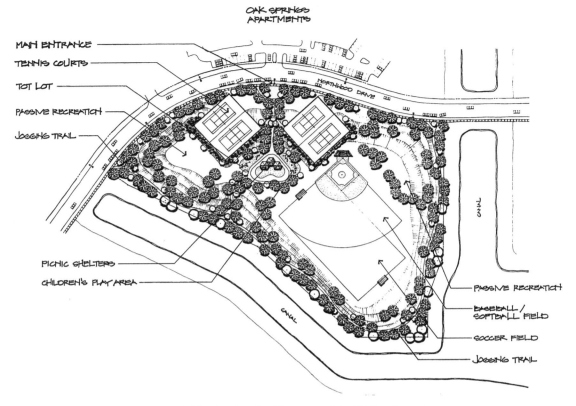

OAK SPRINGS
APARTMENTS

MAIN ENTRANCE

TENNIS COURTS

TOT LOT

PASSIVE RECREATION

JOGGING TRAIL

NORTHWOOD DRIVE

CANAL

PICNIC SHELTERS

CHILDREN'S PLAY AREA

CANAL

PASSIVE RECREATION

BASEBALL /
SOFTBALL FIELD

SOCCER FIELD

JOGGING TRAIL

**Sketch 9.1** Typical suburban neighborhood park. (*Courtesy of the Talbot Group*)

flooded with Saturday morning soccer leagues and softballers and the latter are usually so remote, inhospitable, or environmentally sensitive as to be unusable.

Rarely is there a place in suburban development where one can go to simply be outside, enjoy nature and perhaps picnic. And that's the problem: too much emphasis has been placed on the active recreation areas that are used by a limited number of people for a limited amount of time and otherwise the areas go unused. This is not only insensitive to a broad range of people, it is inefficient use of commonly held land.

However, as the population ages and we hang up our cleats and begrudgingly bequeath our ball gloves to the next generation, it is almost certain that open space will take on an additional role and form, one that is much closer to what Burnham and Olmsted had in mind. Therefore, a different approach to the way we view recreation and open space will be needed to ensure that we are adequately addressing the wishes, desires, and needs of the future. To do this, we must reassess our thinking with regard to recreation and open space in terms of programming, location, and design.

## Programming Aspects

- All ages and segments of society should be served in as many ways as possible on all sites. Old, young, active, passive, male, female, rich, and poor should all have something that appeals to them in every park setting. Too often, the emphasis is strictly on the number of ballfields or tennis courts that can be fitted into a specific area, to serve a limited clientele. By allowing areas to evolve into a softball complex or skateboard center one segment of users attains dominant numbers over others, who never get to use the site. In addition, this results in specialized locations for specific uses, which means that everyone must access them by vehicle.

- The difference between leisure and recreation must be better understood. Leisure is time and experienced-based, while recreation is activity and space-based. One is aesthetically oriented, the other functionally oriented. We must escape the mentality that equates the two and assumes that the number of fields or courts is a measure of satisfactory leisure pursuits. At present the emphasis is clearly on recreation or functionally oriented activities, and the aesthetically oriented are usually relegated to the rare and difficult-to-access preservation areas. Consequently, the varying needs of the citizenry are not being met in equal proportion.

- Contrary to popular thinking earlier in this century, most people have less leisure and recreation time than the previous generation had and, as a result, there is less park use and less time spent in parks. Economic issues, the dissolution of the traditional family, and the related demands on time are in large part the cause. Simply put, it's just not convenient to utilize the 20-acre, district-sized, and larger parks. For whatever reason—effort, time, convenience, or even fear—these parks may not be used as much as neighborhood parks. Being easier to access, containing more familiar faces, and being more easily monitored because of size and perceived sense of ownership, smaller, more usable neighborhood parks should be emphasized.

- With increasing budgetary constraints impacting practically all municipalities, parks, recreation and open-space allocations are a fraction of what they need to be. However, rather than relying on higher taxes to provide the necessary services, innovative ways of privatizing them must be explored. Neighborhood parks are an especially good opportunity. Most neighborhoods would gladly assume the maintenance responsibilities of their smaller, more intimate parks if given the choice between that or increased taxes. In addition, this would truly foster a sense of ownership and responsibility on the part of the residents which, more likely than not, would result in a lower vandalism rate.

- Good community planning utilizes open space and green areas as defining elements, edges, so to speak, of areas or districts, which provides a sense of movement and transition between them. This not only gives a sense of rhythm and delineation, it enhances the feeling of being in a separate locality, a distinct corner of the world, as it were. Opportunities such as this should be capitalized on by "borrowing" greenspace from golf courses, school grounds, or even cemeteries. Utilizing these visual open spaces are an inexpensive but effective method of fostering a feeling of openness in a community.

■ Of all the things that open space should provide or do for the community, it should pervade the fabric of the community just as other structural systems such as roads and utilities do. It should be continuous, accessible, and visible.

## Locational Aspects

■ Parks and open spaces should be prominently placed so that we are aware of them throughout the day in our normal routine. We should be at least exposed to them as we are to the onerous examples of commercial space that girdle our highways and thoroughfares (see Sketch 9.2). The pleasure gained from viewing parks and open spaces, even at 45 to 50 miles per

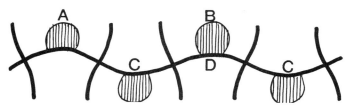

**Sketch 9.2** (**A**) Potential locations of major parks or greenspaces. (**B**) Ideal location is on major thoroughfares and preferably on the outside curve to serve as a focal point. (**C**) Parks should be regularly spaced to create a sense of rhythm to the collector street by "interrupting" other continuous development. (**D**) These locations serve the local neighborhoods while providing an aesthetic view along the collector streets.

**Figure 9.3** Open space should be prominently located. (*Courtesy of the Talbot Group*)

hour, far exceeds the amount of information or convenience to be gained from an equal amount of commercial space and signage.

- All residential areas should be within walking distance of at least a neighborhood park. While it doesn't necessarily need to be located internally, it should be located so that it is visible and easily accessible from the neighborhood in order to serve the area and encourage both its use and pride of ownership in it. Subdivision ordinances usually require a certain amount of recreation space that depends on lot size, but more often than not little guidance is given the developer as to its proper placement. If it is in a convenient, centralized location to the neighborhood and bordered on at least two sides by a public street, it not only serves the public good but is a strong marketing element for home sales (see Sketch 9.3).

- Most people do not live where the major recreational activities occur. Large-scale acquisitions of land for major parks on the fringe of developing suburban areas will never host the number of visitors that most of them are designed to accommodate. With low-density zoning currently serving as the de facto growth control measure in most areas, it is almost assured that relatively few people will ever come into casual contact with these sites and it is practically guaranteed that no form of convenient access, much less mass transit, will ever be available. Instead, communities should concentrate on opportunities closer to the bulk of the population. Besides, preserved farmlands do not constitute an open-space system.

- The location of parks should encourage spontaneous use by visitors. If all parks require premeditation and advanced preparation, much of the enjoy-

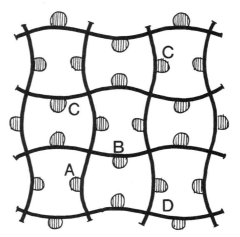

**Sketch 9.3** (**A**) Parks located at their entrances allow pedestrian access from the neighborhoods but also vehicular access from off-site. (**B**) Entrance locations should result in a greater neighborhood sense of pride and ownership, resulting in more regular maintenance. (**C**) If followed areawide, this approach can lead to an evenly distributed system of open spaces. (**D**) With their location along the major thoroughfares, they are more easily monitored and should result in a reduction of undesirable behavior.

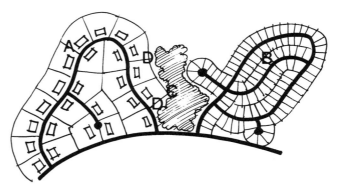

**Sketch 9.4** (**A**) Office development. (**B**) Residential neighborhood. (**C**) Park location serves as an excellent separation and buffering element between differing uses, offering lunchtime activities for the office workers and evening use by the residents. (**D**) Existing parking at the office sites becomes overflow parking during peak weekend residential use.

ment that they can bring is lost. They should be located so as to maximize the interaction with and access to other destinations. Larger parks can become excellent transition spaces between different land uses, but benefit from both. For example, a location between a residential area and an office zone has value to the offices as a convenient lunch place for employees, allows unimpeded evening use by the local residents, and offers ample parking area for peak weekend use (see Sketch 9.4).

- So many parks, especially those adjacent to schools, literally turn their backs on the adjoining streets; some even to the point of walling or fencing them off to inhibit or control access. This seems to defeat the entire purpose of open space and its relationship with the community. A case can be made that not only do these actions not make the space safer, they are just as likely to make it less so. Fewer things are more obtrusive in the landscape than a 6-foot chain link fence surrounding a school site adjacent to a collector road and exposed for all to see.

- Linkages between existing parks need to be identified and actively pursued. These are some of the best opportunities to expand the use of the open space currently in place while expanding access to more residents. In America, most usable land in the suburban areas has been designated for a more productive use than open space, with the exception of the more environmentally sensitive areas, which serve as greenspace buffers. While the recreation potential of these areas is relatively insignificant when considering the number of people who actually use them, nevertheless they do form the framework of what can be a truly integrated, linked, open-space system (see Sketches 9.5a and 9.5b). Working with developers to coordinate the location of any required park space is simple if one takes a broader view or frame of reference than the individual parcel.

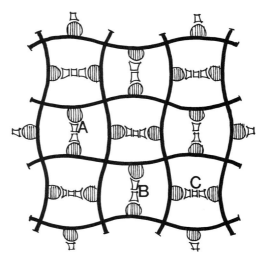

**Sketch 9.5a** (**A**) Linkages between park sites expand the exposure to parks and enhance the usability of sites. (**B**) Connections between park sites may be natural, undevelopable green areas, or may even take the form of lanscaped boulevards. (**C**) Vehicular access through parks should be allowed and encouraged up to a point, to enhance exposure to and convenient use of the areas.

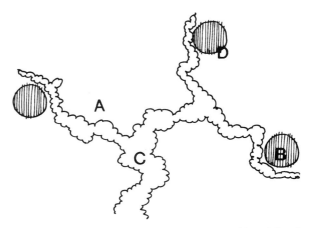

**Sketch 9.5b** (**A**) Naturally occurring greenspace not considered developable for residential or commercial use. (**B**) Potential community park site locations. (**C**) Natural drainage ways, creeks, and changes in grade can provide a ready-made link between recreation areas if they are situated adjacent to them. (**D**) Considered separately, each site and the natural area have limited recreation value and drawing power; considered as a unit, an accessible regional park begins to emerge.

- More parks should be located to reinforce existing and proposed public buildings. Said another way, public buildings and their related greenspaces should be located in more prominent locations so that they become community focal points and activity centers. A new library or recreation center should be a symbol of pride and community, and thus be given an exalted position in the landscape. Too often these are located either on land already owned or cheaply acquired. Fiscal restraint is certainly in order but not at the expense of loss of respect for these extremely significant and rarely built structures. We shouldn't miss such opportunities to reinforce community pride. So often these highly visible sites are designated for commercial use, as they probably should be. However, in some cases a compromise could and should be in order. Important civic structures and their supporting open spaces can be designed into and be made part of an overall commercial area. Just a little more attention to site design will produce spaces that help support one another. There are literally tens of thousands of examples of how this can be sensitively accomplished. They are found all over small-town America (see Sketch 9.6).

## Design Aspects

- Not nearly enough emphasis is being given to the visual and aesthetic consideration of parks. So often they assume the form of very utilitarian spaces offering only ballfields, fenced tennis courts, and unscreened parking areas. More landscape design needs to be incorporated to make these spaces inviting, appealing, and hospitable. Again, the emphasis should be on quality, not necessarily quantity.
- All park and recreation design should be approached using the same design elements utilized for larger-scale community design, namely paths, edges, districts, nodes, and landmarks. They are the basic building blocks of any

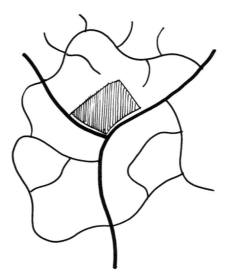

**Sketch 9.6** Highly visible sites deserve a use befitting their location in the neighborhood. Very often these become commercial sites, but many should be designated as public open spaces for use as civic or community structures. With sensitive design, these civic structures and open spaces can even be incorporated with commercial.

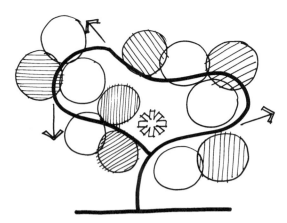

**Sketch 9.7**   In all parks, the spaces and uses should blend and flow one into the other, with just as much emphasis on aesthetics as functionality.

land planning and should be followed. An aesthetic functionalism should be perceived on the part of the user. The experience of a park should occur in a natural, orderly flow, one use area blending harmoniously into the next (see Sketch 9.7).

- As in all design, a park should have a focal point, a theme, a center, a heart, a reason for its existence; it must be desirable before anything else. Be it a view of the ocean, an ancient stand of trees, or merely a meticulously kept azalea garden, all parks must have an underlying purpose to give them significance; simply put, so the people will know they've arrived when they get there.

- Parks that possess activity areas should be designed with both the player, or performer, and the spectator in mind. Albert Rutledge, in his book *A Visual Approach to Park Design,* likens a park to a theater and each of its activity areas to a potential stage.[11] Formal as well as subtle positions for each must be provided, one for display, and one for viewing. In addition, where size permits, viewing the activities from afar is also desirable as it permits one to enjoy the activity without becoming a part of it.

- To better utilize the space available, it is wise to bring activities together where possible, but there should also be subtle screening and buffering. This allows various activities simultaneously, creating a sense of activity and excitement, a "hot spot," if you will, while not letting one dominate the other. Conversely, too much space between activities has a dissipating effect overall and dilutes the sense of activity.

- Parks are to be used by people; therefore, the scale of the space should always relate to human dimensions. Seat heights, walkway widths, seating arrangements, and plaza areas all must feel comfortable to the people using them as well as relate to the scale of the entire space (see Sketches 9.8 and 9.9).

[11]Albert Rutledge. *A Visual Approach to Park Design,* New York: Garland Publishing, Inc., 1981.

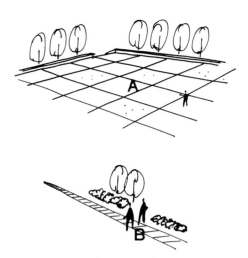

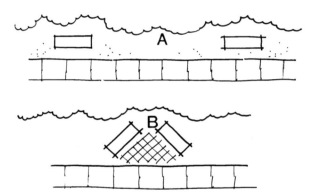

**Sketch 9.8** In all parks the scale of the space should fit the use. (**A**) A plaza, while technically an open space, does not necessarily ensure a pleasant or useful space. (**B**) A path should accommodate the number of people anticipated.

**Sketch 9.9** (**A**) A static and sterile location of park benches does not encourage social interaction. (**B**) A pleasant, recessed niche that encourages conversation by allowing face-to-face conversation can be created just as easily as not.

Seating orientation is particularly important in creating a pleasurable space for conversation and privacy. To maximize people's ability to associate in small groups, benches should be coupled or otherwise oriented to encourage a face-to-face arrangement. This does not mean they must be squarely in front of one another, but somehow the benches and their associated space should form a nook or recess off the walkway. The feeling of privacy should be easily achievable in any park design.

- Park design should always respond to user needs, not necessarily to what the designer thinks is important to include in the plan. There isn't a better recipe for disaster than providing something the people don't want or need.

- According to Rutledge there are eight design goals that every park must satisfy in order to be successful:

   1. Everything must have a purpose. A professor once told me that a designer can do anything that he or she desires as long as it can be justified and defended. There is no room for superfluous uses; all must address an identified need.

   2. Design must be for people. Too much reliance on standards for maintenance equipment, parking requirements, numbers and types of play equipment, and so on, all begin to depersonalize and homogenize the space.

   3. Both function and aesthetic must be satisfied. Neither should take precedence over the other. A balance is in order; efficiency and desirability are achievable simultaneously.

   4. A substantial experience must be established. Nothing should be just randomly placed. Using the elements of design, various feelings or moods should be evoked. The park should become a composition in itself.

   5. An appropriate experience should be established. In a word, context. The design should fit the site; it should blend with and reinforce its surroundings.

   6. Technical requirements must be satisfied. Standard playing field and court sizes should be utilized. A proper orientation and number of activities are required for success.

   7. Needs must be met at the lowest possible cost. Cost benefit analysis should determine priorities. Attention to site constraints allows more efficient design.

   8. Ease of supervision should be provided. Logical and orderly arrangement of activities, linked with an easily understood circulation system, reduces conflicts.

## Summary

Parks and public open spaces need to be thought of more in terms of being integral parts of the community; in fact, they should be considered our communities' primary organizing elements. In past societies they were, and the formula served humanity well for over 8000 years. In the continuum of human existence, our social and physical planning experiments over the last 75 to 100 years are but a moment in time and will be recorded as simply another swing of the pendulum.

The ancients knew and understood the importance and benefit that a well-ordered and functional arrangement of circulation, structure, and open space provided to civilization. They give testimony that there are an almost infinite number of ways that these three elements can be combined while still adhering to certain basic design tenets that create a community with common goals, aspirations, and beliefs. They understood that open space is not negative space or a void, but rather that it is tangible and can be formed to create certain feelings, and it is elemental to the existence of community.

# CHAPTER 10

# Put It
# All Together

Although the majority of Americans now live in cities or suburban areas, if given a choice most would probably opt for a smaller, more intimate setting, a *hometown* wherein they are known and they know their neighbors. In the modern suburban setting we are acquainted with a great many people: the young lady at the grocery store checkout, the cleaning person at the office, the person who takes our quarters at the tollbooth; you get the idea. We recognize many people, but do we know them? Not really; nor they us. Not like the people in a small New England village, a midsized, midwestern prairie town, or even a slow, sleepy southern railroad company town. In these, the scale of the community has not grown to the point of overwhelming the individual. In these, the car is a convenience, not a requirement. In fact, it is still possible to walk from one end to the other in a reasonable time. A Burlington, Vermont, an Annapolis, Maryland, a Williamsburg, Virginia, or an Aspen, Colorado, could never be built using today's standard zoning codes. The places that come to mind when thinking of walkable, memorable community are practically unknown in and around our urban centers.

"Put it all together" implies a certain directed assuredness, a cognitive, knowledgeable approach in planning the built environment; it implies making something whole or complete. In this context it appears that our growth areas have not benefited from such a proactive approach; instead, they've been left to grow like so much mold in a petri dish consuming its host environment. Most areas surrounding our urban centers have no clear goal of development, no vision of what they could and should become. Most are simply designated as an agricultural or very-low-density single-family *holding district* awaiting its time for rezoning to its highest and best use.

Don't misunderstand; the free market is by far the wisest and most effective way to develop property. We certainly don't advocate a central planning authority that attempts to dictate market desires; but it does appear that more expansive thinking on the part of municipal planners is needed to articulate development potentialities that place a higher value on human habitability than on ease of automobile access. That's not to say that they can't coexist, for they certainly can; it just takes a little more effort.

## Development Patterns

### Typical

History tells us what pattern in which development *will* occur if left to its own devices. The typical pattern initially begins with *leapfrog low-density residential* occurring in primarily agricultural districts. As more and more subdivisions are completed, traffic on the local *farm-to-market* two-lane rural roads becomes increasingly congested, resulting in road improvements by the municipality to ease congestion. These improvements, in turn, make the area more desirable for higher-density residential, which continues to occur until the traffic counts warrant rezoning a parcel for a shopping center at one or two of the intersecting farm-to-market roads.

This pattern continues until the principal road in the area is bordered by almost continuous commercial and office development, with successive bands of multi-family, medium-density and low-density residential areas away from the roadway. Most of the traffic from these developments is channeled directly to the major collector road, formerly the farm-to-market road, with little, if any, parallel access to it. That is, there usually is no viable alternative access between two points save for the collector road that connects them, and we all know what can happen when a single traffic signal malfunctions at rush hour (see Sketch 10.1).

With this reliance on such a hierarchical street pattern and the accumulation of ever more traffic on fewer and fewer roads, it's only natural that commercial creeps into the rural transitional areas, lured by the promise of increasing traffic counts.

### Alternative

Our communities need to be designed for the pedestrian experience at 3 to 4 miles an hour, as well as that of the commuter at 35 to 45 miles an hour. It can be done if a two-tiered circulation system that separates local traffic from through traffic is established and an emphasis on a concentration and mixture of land uses at major intersections is not just encouraged but required.

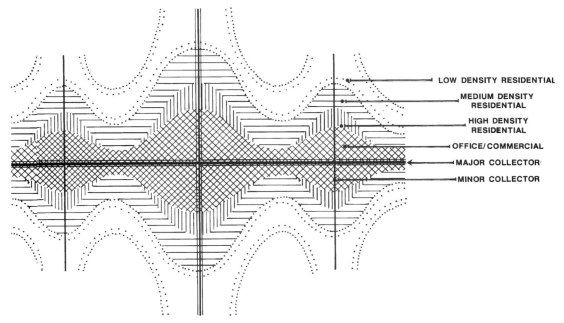

LOW DENSITY RESIDENTIAL

MEDIUM DENSITY
RESIDENTIAL

HIGH DENSITY
RESIDENTIAL

OFFICE/COMMERCIAL

MAJOR COLLECTOR

MINOR COLLECTOR

**Sketch 10.1** Development patterns—typical. (**A**) Continuous office/commercial occurs along the primary corridors. (**B**) Primary intersections encourage major concentrations of commercial. (**C**) Successive bands of multifamily, medium-density, and low-density residential evolve behind the primary corridor. (**D**) To access commercial concentrations, all residential traffic must utilize the collector streets, as no other alternate route exists. (**E**) Increasing traffic requires constant upgrading of collector streets, which, in turn, attracts more traffic. (**F**) Continued sprawl along the collector streets is the ultimate result of this approach.

Beginning with the solutions discussed in Chapter 7, "Where We Spend," and building on them to include high-, medium-, and low-density residential in close proximity to each other, as well as to the commercial and office areas, we can begin to establish a new *planning paradigm,* to replace that found in growth areas today. This new paradigm could be easily adopted as a preferred method of development in the comprehensive planning documents of practically all municipalities (see Sketch 10.2). By graphically identifying preferred locations around major intersections and not necessarily limiting their applicability, the time, energy, and expense of many rezoning battles could be eliminated or at least reduced.

If articulated in this manner, developers and citizens alike would possess a much clearer picture of what the goals of development are. The result: a richer mixture of uses; an emphasis on streets and the pedestrian experience; in short, the creation of small-scale, easily identifiable communities within the context of the larger municipality and not just another *Planned Unit Development* or large-scale subdivision. The beauty of this concept is that it could easily occur relatively quickly, as it requires no wholesale revision of existing zoning or subdivision ordinances.

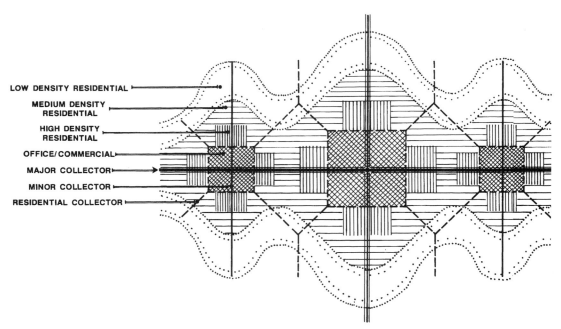

LOW DENSITY RESIDENTIAL
MEDIUM DENSITY RESIDENTIAL
HIGH DENSITY RESIDENTIAL
OFFICE/COMMERCIAL
MAJOR COLLECTOR
MINOR COLLECTOR
RESIDENTIAL COLLECTOR

**Sketch 10.2** Development patterns—alternate. (**A**) Concentrating commercial at the primary intersections and limiting its expansion capability creates a confined commercial district. (**B**) Multi-family areas hold the commercial in place and provide high-density housing within easy walking distance. (**C**) Residential collector street channels local traffic to the office/commercial areas without conflicting with the through traffic on the primary collector streets. (**D**) Secondary loop street around the office/commercial allows convenient local traffic movement without mixing with the through traffic at the primary intersection. (**E**) With the commercial and high-density residential focused at the primary intersections, the intervening lower-density residential and/or greenspaces create a sense of rhythm between the nodes and help to establish a separate identity for each.

## Regional Application

While we recognize that it is not the role of municipal planners to *plan* individual properties and it shouldn't be, it is their role to determine the areas of future growth and the intensity, timing, and sequence of that growth. Many comprehensive plans prepared by municipalities lack a clear vision of a region and its ultimate physical organization. Too often these plans are little more than a patchwork quilt of various zoning districts superimposed over a property line or tax map, rendering few if any concrete conclusions and leaving one rather baffled as to the proper development of an area.

This intentional vagueness in comprehensive planning is the fallacy of the effort. Unless specific target plans are developed for each geographically identifiable zone within a jurisdiction, true planning has not taken place, only policy formulation. In addition, if these target plans are not reinforced with specific design guidelines that depict a preferred method or structure of development, then the typical scenarios with all of their accompanying pitfalls will result.

Only through a process of physical analysis of a region, which identifies the attributes, opportunities, constraints, and ambience, can a true potential image for an area emerge. The natural boundaries of an area should be acknowledged and accentuated to reinforce its unique identity and to ascertain the logical future development nodes and their degree of importance for the area.

These nodes or town centers are the key elements that give a region an identity and are precisely what's lacking in suburbia. However, they could be built by private development if landowners, property developers, engineers, and architects were provided the development goals and incentives for action. Like the smaller cities discussed earlier, these town centers should contain all aspects of a community: schools, libraries, government offices, cultural facilities, houses of worship, offices, commercial, residential, and recreational. While all these features currently exist in suburban districts, usually they are distributed across such a wide area that they possess no sense of focus or connection. However, with the establishment of a strong conceptual framework of design that assures a thematic continuity of structures, these centers would be instantly valuable and desirable as locations, and could easily be sized to accommodate the anticipated population as determined by the regional analysis.

Rethinking our established circulation patterns is another factor that can greatly enhance movement of people and vehicles in and around these nodal centers. As we have seen, most suburban development occurs on a project-by-project basis, employing a minimum number of access points to the local collector streets, with few if any street ties to adjacent properties. Usually commercial zoning and development end up filling the gaps between residential entry points and the primary intersections. The result is heavy traffic on all of the local collector streets, for they are carrying 100 percent of the off-site residential trips simply because there is no other alternative (see Sketch 10.3).

However, by applying the circulation patterns evident at the city or regional scale, along with the separation of local and through traffic discussed earlier to this smaller nodal scale, an easing of traffic problems can certainly be realized. "Mini" beltways around major intersections provide alternate access to the major thoroughfares, and they create additional valuable property for not only office and commercial but medium- to high-density residential as well. This system can result in local collector streets that contain fewer travel lanes carrying less traffic, while a network of residential parkways containing no commercial activity provides an alternative means of access to the commercial areas. Considering the cost of highway construction and land acquisition to accommodate larger and larger collector street rights-of-way, fewer tax dollars would need to be spent in this manner. With this system the residential collector system costs can and should be borne by the individual developers. All that is required for this to happen is for the municipality to adopt development guidelines that state this desire with regard to new residential construction (see Sketch 10.4).

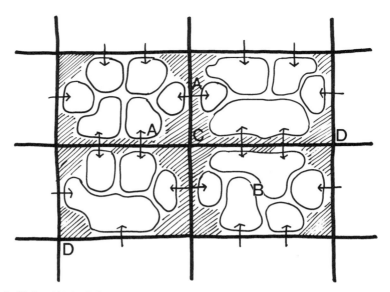

**Sketch 10.3** (**A**) Individual residential sites are developed at different times and usually possess their own "identity" entrance. (**B**) Normally, only indirect street ties between residential areas occur. (**C**) Commercial development occurs at the major intersections and creeps into those areas between and in front of the residential areas. (**D**) Practically all off-site traffic is directed to the local collector streets.

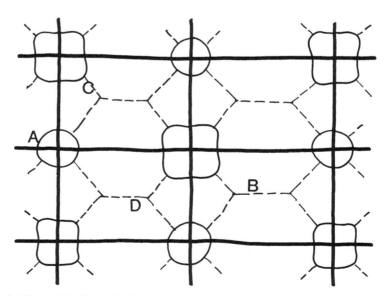

**Sketch 10.4** (**A**) If mini-beltways are provided around the primary intersections, local traffic can be siphoned off the major collector intersections, freeing them for through traffic. (**B**) Residential collector system allows access to the primary intersections and the commercial concentrations without utilizing the major collectors. (**C**) Additional local traffic entering the mini-beltway from the residential collector enhances land values for commercial in the area. (**D**) With the residential collector in place, fewer travel lanes are needed in the major collectors, thus reducing construction costs.

If we can apply the *beltway* concept found around most urban centers to this smaller scale, what other *city* design features can also be applied to make suburban centers functional as well as appealing? When examined, there are several, and perhaps many, commonalities of cities that could serve a useful purpose in designing suburban centers:

- Radiating streets emanating from the city center literally pull the hinterlands inward and serve to anchor the city to its surroundings. Suburban centers are usually approached via one or two collector streets.

- Grand boulevards provide the dual function of direct traffic flow and an active living environment for the residents. Grand parking lots are the suburban equivalent.

- A gridded system of streets provides multiple travel options at the heart of most urban areas. In suburbia, hierarchical street systems direct all traffic to a few specific points.

- A strong street orientation of the buildings creates a reassuring and continuous edge for the pedestrian and motorist alike. Visually uncontained spaces, deep building setbacks filled with asphalt parking areas, and large, low-level monolithic structures make suburban centers inhospitable.

- A mixture of uses in close proximity to one another, in most cases over one another, creates a vibrant energy lacking in all but a few suburban mixed-use developments. The separation of land uses into various zones of similarity requires automobile access between them; although this robs the street of pedestrian use, it is the normal situation in suburbia today.

While these are just a few salient points that highlight the difference between proven community planning principles and those in use today, it is obvious that conscious, objective planning is either not occurring or is ineffective in creating environments scaled for the individual and responsive to the human experience. Instead, the quality communities being built today are done so at the direction of enlightened developers or progressive corporations in spite of the restrictions placed on them by zoning, subdivision, and site plan ordinances. By amassing large landholdings they can literally create their own community with the appropriate land use mixes, the right emphasis on construction detailing, and an unswerving focus on a goal.

## Site Application

What are these singularly focused individuals and groups doing that our municipal planners either can't do or are not allowed to do? Is it simply a matter of scale differences or the lack of a true understanding on the part of our hired, appointed, and elected officials as to the nature of community? A rhetorical question to be sure, and an answer to which won't be found here. What we will do is to attempt to annotate some universal design solutions that seem to be working.

*New Solutions*

- *A rejection of euclidean zoning as the only approach to suburban design.*
That wholesale separation of uses has probably created more problems than
it attempted to solve. In its beginning there was a logical, defendable reason for its use. With smokestack industries lying adjacent to single-family
housing districts, "sweatshop" factories so tightly packed as to become fire
hazards, and many more such examples abounding, there was a need. Now,
this form of zoning merely separates one socioeconomic strata from another and all housing from its dependent commercial areas. As Sketch 10.5
depicts, it is possible and feasible to include a variety of housing types, as
well as office and commercial uses, all in close proximity to one another
and served by an interconnected road system to encourage interaction and
access. With this basic concept it's possible to completely separate through
traffic from local traffic without the need of limited access highways and
grade-separated interchanges.

- *The concept of a town center as opposed to a shopping center as the community commercial, office, and social focus.* A shopping center implies
typical retail uses such as a grocery store, pizza parlor, dry cleaner, and an
outparcel or two containing a fast-food franchise and a self-serve gas station. A town center, on the other hand, brings to mind a complex mix of
divergent uses: office, retail, civic, cultural, housing, and even light industry, in a defined, centralized area, visually and physically well connected to

**Sketch 10.5** Commercial, offices, apartments, townhouses, and medium- and low-
density housing can all occur in a confined area and be served by a continuous, interconnected street network. A logical, orderly progression of land uses can coexist without the normal zoning "bandaids" of setbacks, landscaping, and fences. Instead, streets
and alleys serve as the transitional elements.

its supportive areas. A town center implies a certain excitement, enchantment, and "electricity" generated from chance meetings and unexpected occurrences that result from such an urban bazaar. Sketch 10.6, a variation of Sketch 10.5, expresses how adaptable this form is to an entire quadrant of an intersection. If this idea is replicated in the remaining quadrants (Sketch 10.7), the image of a small town emerges. Granted, this is an idealized "crystallized" form; nevertheless it represents a structure that begins to establish a *town center* concept of development as opposed to the typical strip commercial, isolated subdivision form.

- *The elimination of typical strip commercial as an acceptable land use within the boundaries of the community.* While there is an acknowledgement of the need for this kind of commercial activity, there is also a growing recognition that the form of the structure, and not the use, is the negative factor. A greater emphasis on design and an understanding that visibility is not the requirement that most commercial real estate agents profess. Any enclosed mall is a good example of this fact. As Sketch 10.8 shows, an acceptable combination of off-site oriented and internally oriented commercial can be achieved in a neighborhood setting. While this may not fit the ideal of the previous examples, it does reflect a realistic transition to that ideal, an adaptation to circumstances, as it were. This gives us encouragement that in the case of awkward, land-locked, and passed-over parcels, more innovative forms of planning can still be applied to create environments better that the typical or expected one.

- *The utilization of a more formal arrangement in the siting and layout of streets and the organization of spaces.* At higher densities and more intense uses, curved streets begin to lose their effectiveness and efficiency. They are literally more at home in low- to mid-density residential areas. Curvilinear streets denote a sense of privacy and separation, while a grid system implies openness, accessibility, and connectedness. No longer are symmetry and balance dirty words in planning parlance. On the contrary, the public and planners alike seem to be rediscovering the implied structure, order, and perceptibility this form of neighborhood design imparts. In addition, a grid system is more easily understood and more predictable than a curvilinear pattern, which by its very nature is confusing, confounding, and unpredictable.

- *More streets considered usable and frontable.* Unlike a hierarchical system that places housing on only the smallest streets and relegates the larger collector streets to access and circulation, there is a growing tendency to utilize a greater portion of all roadways and streets as land uses that are productive and directly accessible to all. This leads to less street being required to serve land area and number of units. Lower initial development costs and reduced maintenance costs for the municipality result in more affordable housing. A pleasant by-product is the homeowners' sense of ownership of and responsibility for the attendant streets.

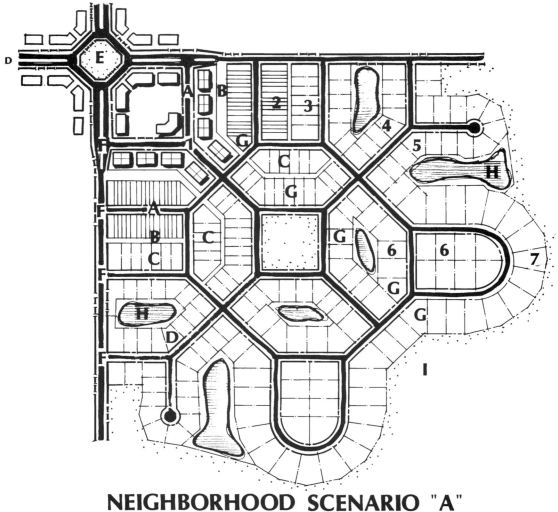

# NEIGHBORHOOD SCENARIO "A"
## PUBLIC SEWER & WATER

**Sketch 10.6** (**A**) Apartment/condo flats and street-oriented townhouses with parking and garages to rear of unit enhance streetscape. (**B**) Rear parking provides secure resident parking and on-street visitor parking. (**C**) Street-oriented 3500- to 6000-square-foot single-family lots with alleyway and rear-garage resident parking continues the streetscape. (**D**) Single-family lots, 7500+ square feet, are smallest to be allowed front-loaded garages to reduce cluttered driveway parking. (**E**) Traffic circle or diamond creates community focal point and reinforces pedestrian environment while providing opportunity for statuary, other artwork, or landscape elements. (**F**) Multiple access points from through road allow direct access to the various housing types, enhancing marketability. (**G**) Gradual transition of housing options from apartment/condo to 20,000+-square-foot lots without restrictive zoning lines helps establish a less stratified neighborhood. (**H**) Stormwater retention areas are located to enhance lot values, expand open space, and provide interconnected stormwater management systems with multiple outfall options. (**I**) Recreational/visual amenities such as golf courses, regional lake system, equestrian/jogging trails, etc., serve as the edge delineator of the village, prohibiting unchecked expansion. (*Courtesy of the Talbot Group*)

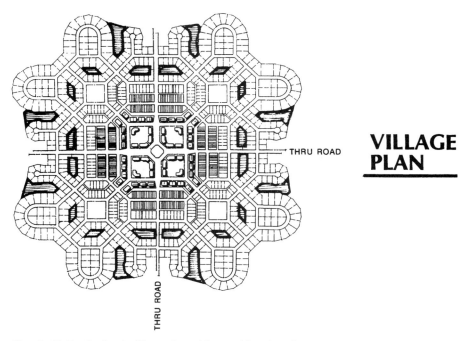

THRU ROAD

THRU ROAD

# VILLAGE PLAN

**Sketch 10.7**   Stylized village plan with transitional zoning.

- *A rediscovery of the alley as a civilizing community element.*   The reintroduction of the alley is allowing an alternative to the garage-door-dominant streetscape typical of suburban areas. This technique is being effectively used in townhouse developments and smaller, higher-density, single-family areas, resulting in a reduction in the amount of paving at the front of the dwelling, a firmer streetscape edge, more available visitor parking, less street congestion and generally a more aesthetically pleasing visual environment.

- *Conscious attempts to reduce the negative impacts of the omnipresent automobile in new developments.*   With the mushrooming of car ownership in the last 15 or 20 years, it is no longer possible to simply treat with disdain their presence in our midst; we must actively pursue more sensitive and innovative methods of accommodating them. All elements of community design, from landscape screening to highway geometrics, are being reexamined as to their primary and secondary roles in serving the community, and are being modified if, in their strict adherence to typical standards, they are found to undermine the concept of community.

- *A greater emphasis on and concern for the fabric of the street; that is, a realization that the structures should face and address the street to possess a true street address.*   Whether they are housing, commercial, or office, buildings must be thought of as part of a continuous street edge, vertical walls that contain the street and enclose the space. Too many gaps or breaks in this "wall" weaken the ability of the remaining structures to create that

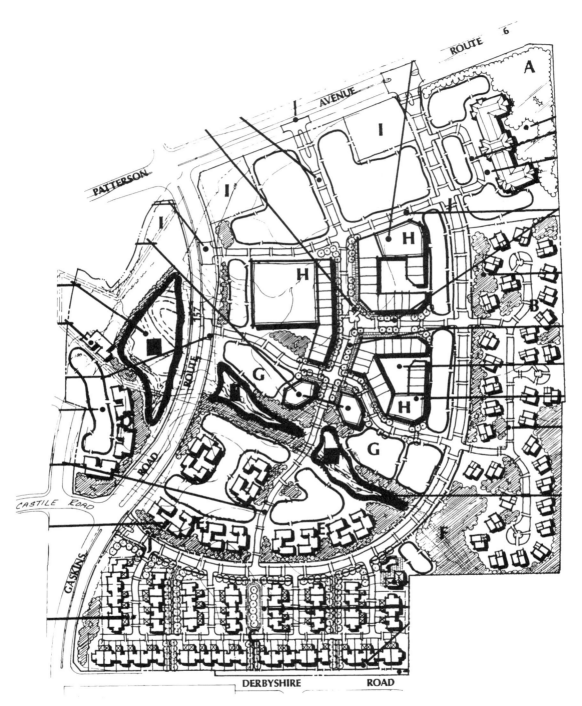

**Sketch 10.8** Neighborhood concept utilizing transitional zoning techniques. (*Courtesy of the Talbot Group*)

**Figure 10.1**   Reintroduction of the alley.

desirable sense of place. Only in this manner does a street take on a true character, a unique spatial quality of livability; otherwise it becomes just another lifeless collector street.

■ *An increased understanding of what the scale and texture of a building has on a street and what an important role each plays in creating interesting and enjoyable spaces.*   While monolithic walls and slick, glass-skinned structures take on a sculptural quality when seen from a distant expressway at 65 miles per hour, from the adjacent sidewalk these structures appear cold, aloof, and fortresslike—strangely alien constructs apparently designed for beings larger than ourselves. New designs, on the other hand, are showing detail, celebrating changes in texture, utilizing more common and familiar materials, and going to great lengths to establish a sense of repetition and depth through the effective use of seam patterns, reveals, cornices, bases, and finials.

■ *Much less emphasis on the separation of pedestrians and vehicles.*   It is widely accepted that this 1970s planning concept that encouraged linear greenbelts throughout residential areas has resulted in some very dull and boring streetscapes and, in as many cases as not, some very real safety concerns for the residents adjacent to them. Quite the contrary, today the street is to be celebrated and enjoyed as a place for community interaction, with the rear yard to be enjoyed by close friends and family and out of the casual view of the passing public.

■ *A new respect for contextualism in civic architecture, commercial structures, and residential dwellings.*   As community planners, we need to champion this recognition by reinforcing the principle that community comprises all the structures that occur within its bounds and that interest and variety is possible while a theme or a predominant building style is adhered to. Overwhelming, out of place, or outlandish architectures serve to rend the community, not reinforce it.

■ *An understanding that gradual transitions of land uses and densities are necessary to create the perception of a center or focus for the community.*

One use should blend into another in an orderly, organized progression that builds to a crescendo: *the 100 percent place.* Unlike current planning which relies on sudden, harsh, and abrupt changes in zoning and land use and requires all manner of landscape screening and buffering devices to divide and separate areas, new communities should be designed to allow a variety of housing types and commercial structures within the context of a continuous street network that culminates in the center of the community (see Sketch 10.9).

- *Different uses within the same building, one over the other, are not a negative but create a more interesting and healthy economic environment.* Increasingly more people are beginning to believe this, contrary to what the planning profession has preached for the last 30 to 40 years. While we're all familiar with the giant, glowing multiuse megastructures occurring in most urban situations in America, the point to be made here is that developers and land planners want more intimately scaled low- to mid-rise structures that provide small offices and apartments or condominiums over street-oriented commercial. While this form is common in the small towns that came of age in the nineteenth century, it appears to be fairly radical for suburbia.

- *Parks and open spaces designed as the front lawn of the community; places to be designed for and enjoyed by people of all ages.* They should offer more than just ballfields, play areas, and parking lots. They should be spaces that are truly designed for a purpose and not just leftover parcels that couldn't be served by gravity sewer lines. These prominently dis-

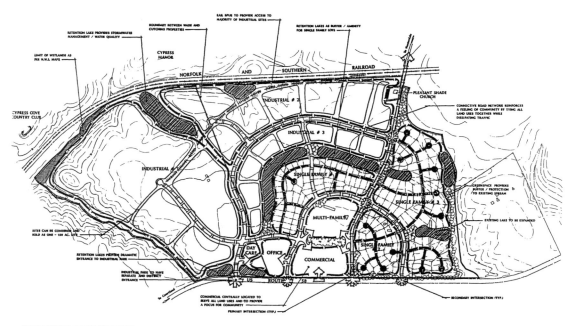

CONCEPTUAL LAND USE PLAN

**Sketch 10.9** Neighborhood concept utilizing transitional zoning techniques. (*Courtesy of the Talbot Group*)

played, proactively designed community spaces serve both to separate and connect. They should complete or frame the views, act as dignified or classical parks to complement civic architecture, function as community celebration areas, or merely be a quiet oasis where one can be alone in a crowd.

- *Landscaping understood as something more than just so much greenery to be used to pretty up the place.* Size, habit, texture, color, massing possibilities, design suitability, and aesthetic quality are merely a few of the factors that should be applied to trees as they relate to community structure and the articulation of open space. They should be utilized to delineate space effectively, to direct attention to some focal point, be used as buffer enhancement and transitional elements, in addition their obvious use in providing shade. Plant material, from the ground on up, is truly the glue that holds it all together.

- *A greater attempt to anchor new development to its site surroundings using local lore, indigenous architecture, and building materials reflecting the surrounding development patterns.* Attention to these details vis-à-vis the local color can easily determine the success or failure of a development, as it is extremely important to reinforce the image of the existing community, not conflict with it.

These "new" solutions are not the complete answer; on the contrary, they are a meager beginning to addressing the problems so pervasive in our suburban growth areas. These solutions, and all the ideas and concepts presented in this book, are intended to promote the fact that there is a glaring and growing problem resulting from the standard method of development, and to express practical, and in most cases, practiced techniques of community development.

## Summary

Our current approach to planning our suburban areas is failing. It has begun to create more problems than it has solved. A half century ago our planners rejected many of the practical and proven methods of community building that had worked for mankind for millennia. In our rush to adapt to the new transportation age, we virtually threw the baby out with the bathwater.

What has resulted is a landscape of sprawl and chaos. We have allowed our transportation requirements to define the structure of our cities, and have situated the various community elements along the arteries like so many separate and distinct monocultures of activity. We have relegated the noble profession of planning to mere site-plan review, in which the primary concern and result is screening, buffering, or otherwise hiding one use area from another. With such a focus on detail, little true planning appears to be taking place, merely processing.

While it is true that municipal planners are charged with identifying long-range population trends and projections and the physical infrastructure required to support such populations, and they do that well, there exists a wide chasm between these two extremes of mega and minutia that isn't being addressed. Between the visionary scale (long-range comprehensive planning) and the realist scale (site-plan review), the concept of community resides. It is in this realm that change can be best effected, by establishing defined goals and parameters to determine how the developing areas will function, how the various elements will fit together to create something more than just so many separate shopping centers, offices, and parks strewn around an intersection. This book attempts to identify some potential solutions to common problems evident in this range and, hopefully, to affect the thinking of all the players involved in community building.

A reexamination of what constitutes a community and a reassessment of what form or forms might better serve it in the future are in order. The authors are not municipal planners per se, but we do actively participate in the planning process in our attempt to create communities, and in that effort we see a growing frustration, a dissatisfaction, a sense of powerlessness on the part of planners to produce the kind of quality environments they know are possible. As stated in Chapter 1, we must reacquaint ourselves with the physical attributes of a community and, by organizing them on a conceptual basis, truly design our communities. Any designer, whether an architect, engineer, or landscape architect, must conceive a plan in response to a client's wishes and desires and articulate that plan so that it can be easily understood and eventually constructed. Where this situation differs from the community building process of our municipal planners is that there is follow-through on the concept to reality. A great many professional planners today are more involved in policy formation and goal setting, but allow others to complete the process to reality. In order for planners to be effective in the future, they must go beyond policy and goal issues; they must take the process to the next step: design conceptualization. They need not prepare specific plans for specific areas, but they must give graphic expression to the preferred reality as generally stated in the goals, objectives, and policy. Unless every planning document contains preferred methods and standards of development that clearly convey a desired future, the future will be merely an up-to-date version of the present chaos and sprawl.

We must recognize that a community is more than the sum of its parts. When properly conceived, it provides for all the needs of its inhabitants within a geographically identifiable area and instills in them a sense of identity and belonging. A community must impart to all who are exposed to it a particular image of itself, a unique and individual character recognizable among others. Its various elements complement and support one another by functioning interactively. In short, a community should bind its people in a common identity, not separate or divide them. Achieving this desirable goal requires a change in our approach to community building; new solutions must be developed, and a new vision of suburbia must be mandated.

# Glossary

**Bandaid landscaping**   Landscape screens or planting buffers used to cover up or mitigate poor planning.

**Benchmarks**   A stationary object located by the survey, which can be used as a reference point in the field.

**Boulevard**   A wide, tree-lined street, sometimes referred to as a parkway because of its heavy landscaping.

**Climax species**   The final stage in ecological succession; herein refers to commercial development.

**Conditional zoning**   A variance to a zoning constraint, which allows a use that would otherwise be restricted, in exchange for some guarantee or proffer made by a developer to the municipality. For example: Higher density is allowed on a parcel if open space will be developed at the same time.

**Construction documents**   The plans, details, and elevations or blueprints used for construction.

**Conterminous United States**   The 48 states that share a common boundary.

**Demographics**   The vital statistics and characteristics of human population.

**Detention pond**   An engineered drainage facility designed to collect storm-water for complete gradual discharge.

**Ditch lines**   Drainage ditches.

**Diversity**   A mixture of uses that provides something for everybody, resulting in activity and vitality.

**Dominant element**   An object that because of some overpowering characteristic (i.e., size, color, etc.) commands attention and provides a reference point.

**Easement**   Access rights to a portion of a piece of property for which the owner gives up his rights of development in order that another party (usually government or a utility company) have use for a specific purpose (i.e., a power line).

**Ecosystem**   The dynamic whole produced by the inhabitants of a living habitat.

**Enclosure**   The sensation created by objects in close proximity to one another.

**Final subdivision plan**  An accurate scale representation of a proposed land use.

**Flood plain**  The land area adjacent to a body of water or water course that is subject to inundation.

**Franchise architecture**  Building forms of similar characteristics, colors, and materials that are typical of chain stores and fast-food establishments.

**Friction**  Anything that slows down the flow of automobile traffic, requiring vehicle stops and starts (i.e., intersections, curb cuts, median breaks, mail boxes, etc.).

**Hardsheet**  The mathematically correct drawing that establishes a concept in the two-dimensional plane.

**Hardship**  A burden created when general zoning restrictions prohibit an owner from using his property in the way he wishes.

**Infrastructure**  Streets, storm sewers, pumping stations, sanitary sewer lines, water lines, etc.

**Ingress/egress**  Entrance and exit points.

**Invert**  The top of a drainage pipe below grade.

**Landschaft**  (Medieval) A cluster of dwellings and other buildings immediately surrounded by farm fields, with forest or marsh at the extreme perimeters. The connotation of landschaft to its inhabitants was one of both obligation and responsibility to one another and to the land.

**Light duty road**  A byway used for limited access to some remote area. For example: A road used to access a fire tower.

**Open space**  The non-built environment that provides green relief.

**Parcel**  A portion of a subdivision; a tract or lot.

**Physical survey**  The field location of physical elements and legal boundaries performed by a qualified land surveyor.

**Plan**  A method of action; a way of doing a thing; a drawing or diagram.

**Plat**  A recordable document that gives form and detail substance to a plan.

**Plot**  A two-dimensional hand-drawn or computer-produced graphic.

**Primary highway**  The principal roadway dedicated to vehicular traffic.

**Proffer**  A guarantee made by a developer or owner to provide some kind of service or amenity in exchange for municipal approval of the plan. For example: The developer volunteers to pay for extending municipal infrastructure to his site if project approval is granted by the planning commission.

**Program**  The goals and expectations for a project. The desired behaviors or activities that will occur within the subject site, place, or locale.

**Quadrangle window**  The area captured in the USGS map sheet.

**Retention**  An engineered facility for the collection and storage of stormwater.

**Review board**    Some group whose task it is to review proposed land use (i.e., planning commission, city council, etc.).

**Right-of-way**    The easement dedicated to municipal use on either side of a publicly owned street.

**Rim**    The pavement or grade elevation of a manhole cover or drain inlet.

**Ring road**    The road that forms the outer limits of a shopping mall.

**Scenic easement**    A portion of land on one or both sides of a street that is dedicated to open space or landscaping.

**Secondary highway**    An alternative road to a primary highway. For example: The two-lane business route at an interstate exit.

**Setback**    That required distance measured from the public right-of-way in which no private construction may encroach without prior approval from the municipality.

**Site coverage**    The percentage of a site that is covered by the built environment.

**Stereo pairs**    Two overlapping high-resolution stereoscopic photographs.

**Stereoscopic photographs**    Photographs that appear three dimensional, revealing topographic characteristics when viewed with a stereoscope.

**Subdivision plat**    Recording document that establishes property ownership, utility easements, and public rights-of-way.

**Superelevation**    The cross-slope of a high-speed road that allows a vehicle to safely "hug" the road in a curve.

**Take down**    A portion of a subdivided parcel of land that is bought at a given time.

**Urban sprawl**    Uncontrolled development; unplanned creep into the hinterlands.

**Vertical curve**    The parabolic curve that allows safe and efficient vehicular travel on roads with vertical grade change.

**Watershed**    The land area drained by a stream or river.

# Suggested Readings

Attoe, Wayne, and Donn Logan. *American Urban Architecture, Catalysts in the Design of Cities,* Berkeley, Calif.: University of California Press, 1989.

Beckley, Robert M. "Urban Design," *Introduction to Urban Planning,* edited by Anthony J. Catanese and James C. Snyder, New York: McGraw-Hill, 1979.

Bishop, Kirk W. *Designing Urban Corridors,* Chicago: American Planning Association, 1989.

Boden, Margaret A. *The Creative Mind: Myths and Mechanisms,* London: HarperCollins, 1991.

*Business and Industrial Park Development Handbook,* Washington, D.C.: Urban Land Institute, 1988.

Cervero, Robert. *Suburban Gridlock,* New Brunswick, N.J.: Center for Urban Policy Research, 1986.

Coleman, Richard C. "Sub-Urban Design: Re-creation of a Town Center in the Face of Suburban Growth," in *Urban Design and Preservation Quarterly,* Winter, 1990.

*Cost Effective Site Planning,* Washington, D.C.: National Association of Home Builders, 1976.

Cullen, Gordan. *The Concise Townscape,* New York: Van Nostrand Reinhold, 1961.

DeChiara, Joseph, and Lee Koppelman. *Site Planning Standards,* New York: McGraw-Hill, 1978.

DeChiara, Joseph, *Timesavers Standards for Residential Development,* New York: McGraw-Hill, 1984.

DeChiara, Joseph and Lee Koppelman. *Urban Planning and Design Criteria,* New York: Van Nostrand Reinhold, 1984.

Glaser, Nathan, and Mark Lilla. *The Public Face of Architecture, Civic Culture and Public Spaces,* New York: The Free Press, a Division of Macmillan, Inc., 1987.

Gold, Seymour M. *Recreation Planning and Design,* New York: McGraw-Hill, 1980.

Graves, Maitland. *The Art of Color and Design,* Second Edition, New York: McGraw-Hill, 1951.

Heckscher, August. *Open Spaces, The Life of American Cities,* The Twentieth Century Fund, Inc., New York: Harper & Row, 1971.

Hedman, Richard, and Andrew Jaszewske. *Fundamentals of Urban Design,* Washington, DC: APA Press, 1984.

Howard, Ebenezer. *Garden Cities of Tomorrow,* England: Faber and Faber Ltd., 1965.

Jacobs, Jane. *The Death and Life of Great American Cities,* New York: Random House, 1961.

Kennedy, Robert Woods. *The House and the Art of Its Design,* New York: Reinhold, 1953.

*Land Development Manual,* Washington, D.C.: National Association of Home Builders, 1974.

Laseau, Paul. *Graphic Problem Solving for Architects and Designers,* Second Edition, New York: Van Nostrand Reinhold, 1986.

Lynch, Kevin. *The Image of the City,* Boston: The M.I.T. Press, 1986.

McMahon, John. *Property Development, Effective Decision Making in Uncertain Times,* New York: McGraw-Hill, 1976.

Newman, Oscar. *Defensible Space,* New York: Collier Books, 1973.

*Parking Requirements for Shopping Centers: Summary Recommendations and Research Study Report,* Washington, D.C.: Urban Land Institute, 1982.

Phillips, E. Barbara, and Richard T. LeGates. *City Lights, An Introduction to Urban Studies,* Oxford: Oxford University Press, 1981.

*Planning for Better Housing,* Washington, D.C.: The National Association of Home Builders, 1980.

*Planning for Housing, Development Alternatives for Better Environments*, Washington, D.C.: Special Committee on Land Development, National Association of Home Builders, 1980.

*Residential Development Handbook,* Washington, D.C.: Residential Council, Urban Land Institute, 1978.

*Residential Streets,* Washington, D.C.: Urban Land Institute, American Society of Civil Engineers, National Association of Home Builders, 1974.

Rubenstein, Harvey M. *A Guide to Site and Environmental Planning,* New York: John Wiley & Sons, Inc., 1969.

Rutledge, Albert J. *A Visual Approach to Park Design,* New York: Garland STPM Press, 1981.

Rutledge, Albert J. *Anatomy of a Park, The Essentials of Recreation Planning and Design,* New York: McGraw-Hill, 1971.

Sanders, Welford, Judith Getzels, David Mosena, JoAnn Butler. *Affordable Single-Family Housing,* Washington, D.C.: American Planning Association, 1984.

Sanders, Welford. *Zero Lot Line Development,* Washington, D.C.: American Planning Association, 1982.

Sherderjian, Denise. *Uncommon Genius: How Great Ideas Are Born,* New York: Viking Books, 1990.

*Shopping Center Development Handbook,* Washington, D.C.: Commercial and Office Development Council, Urban Land Institute, 1977.

Simonds, John Ormsbee. *Landscape Architecture, The Shaping of Man's Natural Environment,* New York: McGraw-Hill, 1961.

Skokowski, Henry and Mark Brodeur. "Maintaining the Pedestrian Quality of Small Town Downtowns," *Urban Design and Preservation Quarterly,* Winter 1990.

Tobey, George B. *A History of Landscape Architecture: The Relationship of People to the Environment,* New York: American Elsevier Publishing Company, Inc., 1973.

Todd, Kim W. *Site, Space, and Structure,* New York: Van Nostrand Reinhold, 1985.

Tucker, William. "Revolt in Queens," *The American Spectator,* February 1993.

Untermann, Richard, and Anne Vernez Moudon. "Designing Pedestrian Friendly Commercial Streets," *Urban Design and Preservation Quarterly,* Fall 1990.

Untermann, Richard, and Robert Small. *Site Planning for Cluster Housing,* New York: Van Nostrand Reinhold, 1977.

VanDyke, Scott. *From Line to Design, Design Graphics Communication,* Second Edition, PDA Publishers Corporation, 1985.

Wang, Thomas C. *Plan and Section Drawing,* New York: Van Nostrand Reinhold, 1979.

Wentling, John W., and Lloyd W. Bookout. *Density by Design,* Washington, D.C.: Urban Land Institute, 1988.

Witherspoon, Robert E., Jon P. Abbett, and Robert M. Gladstone. *Mixed Use Developments: New Ways of Land Use.* Washington, D.C.: Urban Land Institute, 1976.

White, William. *The Social Life of Small Urban Spaces,* Washington, D.C.: The Conservation Foundation, 1980.

White, William H. *City, Rediscovering the Center,* New York: Doubleday, a Division of Bantam Doubleday Dell Publishing Group, Inc., 1988.

# Index

## ABOUT THE AUTHORS

GERALD A. PORTERFIELD is director of Community Design for The Talbot Group. He holds a B.S. in landscape architecture, and he is a member of the Urban Land Institute as well as the American Planning Association. He is a frequent speaker on land development issues.

KENNETH B. HALL, JR., ASLA, is a landscape architect with the firm CMSS Architects. He holds a B.S. in history and a master's degree in landscape architecture, and he has published a variety of technical articles focusing on community and park planning.